EXPLORING DURHAM HISTORY

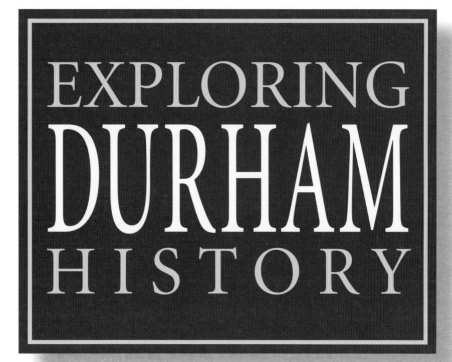

EXPLORING DURHAM HISTORY

PHOTOGRAPHY BY
PHILIP NIXON

WRITTEN BY
PHILIP NIXON
AND
DENIS DUNLOP

The Breedon Books
Publishing Company
Derby

First published in Great Britain by
The Breedon Books Publishing Company Limited
Breedon House, 44 Friar Gate, Derby, DE1 1DA.
1998

ISBN 1 85983 117 6

Printed and finished by Butler & Tanner Ltd,
Selwood Printing Works, Caxton Road, Frome,
Somerset.

Colour separations by Radstock Reproductions,
Somerset.

Cover printing by Lawrence-Allen Colour Printers,
Weston-super-Mare, Avon.

Contents

Dry Stone Walling

Southern County Durham

Index

Introduction

FROM ancient times a succession of evolving inhabitants have left their mark on County Durham. It is a wonderful area and its rich history enjoys what is, possibly, a unique niche.

During the Industrial Revolution, County Durham was at the forefront of mining, railways and heavy industry but a massive change has taken place over the last few years and created what is now, perhaps, one of the most rural counties in England. Even so, this industrial heritage is as much a part of its history as the Bronze Age people with their skills and superstitions and the Romans with their wondrous technology.

In County Durham it is difficult to escape the influence of the mighty Prince Bishops. They enjoyed a power and an independence rare in English history. They raised their own armies and some, such as Anthony Bek, even led their men into battle. They also minted their own coins, passed their own laws, levied their own taxes, granted charters and enjoyed the right of forfeiture. They ruled the bishopric for centuries with a power that was normally enjoyed only by the King himself. Their throne was the highest in Christendom, confirming the position of the Prince Bishop.

These charismatic men were a combination of barons and religious leaders. Their coats-of-arms were surmounted by the mitre-cum-coronet with, depicted behind the shield, a crozier and sword crossed, instead of the crossed croziers that would normally have been a bishop's insignia. As well as religious leaders and warriors they were educators, builders and politicians — powerful men indeed.

County Durham is an area of variety. Its heart is a cathedral city — a city that enjoys all the advantages of a county seat with few of the disadvantages. The city is small enough to be explored on foot, yet it is so magnificent that the cathedral and castle, together with their surrounding buildings, have been designated a World Heritage Site.

Art and culture abound in Durham. The John and Josephine Bowes Museum, housed in a French-style chateau on the edge of the Dales market town of Barnard Castle, is one of the finest treasure houses in Europe. Beamish Museum — winner of many awards — is a step back into the social and industrial history of the region. Killhope is the most complete lead mining site in Britain, where a dramatic reconstruction enables visitors to enjoy, firsthand, a portrayal of the working lives of the North Pennines lead miners.

There are many castles, reminders of more unsettled times, from Durham Castle — University College and home of the Prince Bishops for almost 800 years — to Bowes Castle, a lonely outpost, standing four-square to the elements, guarding the entrance to the wild Stainmore Pass. Churches range from the mighty Norman cathedral, regarded as the most beautiful religious building in the world, to the humble Saxon church at Escomb, one of the finest examples of early Christian architecture in Europe.

County Durham was the birthplace of railways and the early pioneers. The Stephensons and Timothy Hackworth are remembered in the region's famous railway museums. The more mysterious aspect of the county is represented in the folk-tales and legends, such as the Lambton and Sockburn Worms, fanciful, maybe, but still, inextricably, part of the area's fascinating history.

Exploring Durham History selects not only the main subjects in the history of the county, but also highlights some of the less well-known aspects.

This combination will, hopefully, encourage greater interest. We have inherited this county from its previous inhabitants and hope that our presentation would have met with their approval, even though it is offered in a lighter vein. We have a great enthusiasm for our county and hope that this is conveyed through our work.

Although our names are recorded as authors, we do feel that this privilege should be shared with previous generations — the creators of our history — and, of course, all those amenable, approachable County Durham folk who have given their time and effort to help us with this book and to whom we extend our grateful thanks.

Philip Nixon & Denis Dunlop
April 1998

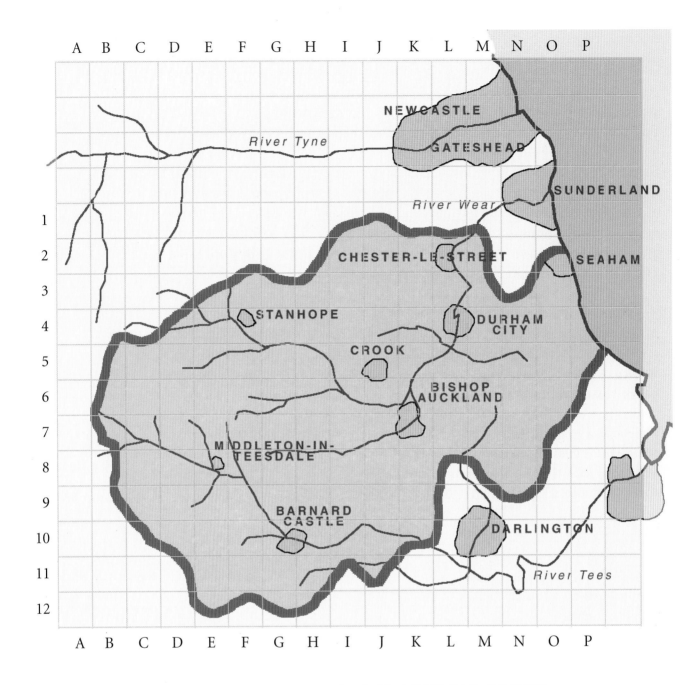

COUNTY DURHAM GEOGRAPHICAL ORDER

DURHAM CITY:
DURHAM CATHEDRAL *L4*
BEDESMENS BENCH *L4*
DUN COW PANEL *L4*
SANCTUARY KNOCKER *L4*
DURHAM CASTLE *L4*
LONDONDERRY STATUE *L4*
NORTH ROAD DRINKING FOUNTAIN *L4*
HOUSE OF CORRECTION *L4*
WATERGATE *L4*
SHIPPERDSON'S COTTAGE *L4*
BANKSMAN'S COTTAGE *L4*
SOUTH STREET MILL *L4*
CHARLEY CROSS *L4*
DLI MUSEUM *L4*
BATTLE OF NEVILLES CROSS *L4*
ALDIN GRANGE BRIDGE *L4*
MAIDEN CASTLE *L4*
TINKLERS LANE *L4*
ST MARY MAGDALENE'S CHAPEL *L4*
VANE TEMPEST HALL *L4*
KEPIER BRICK KILN *L4*
KEPIER QUARRIES *L4*
BELMONT VIADUCT *L4*
BRASSIDE PONDS *L3*
FINCHALE PRIORY *L3*
ST LAWRENCE CHURCH *M4*
BRANCEPETH CASTLE *L5*
CROXDALE HALL *L5*

**EASTERN COUNTY
DURHAM:**
SIGNING BANK *N4*
LUDWORTH TOWER *N4*
HASWELL ENGINE HOUSE *N3*
KELLOE CHURCH *N5*
ST MARY'S CHURCH, TRIMDON *O5*
SHOTTON HALL *P4*
SEATON HOLME *P4*
EASINGTON COLLIERY *P4*
BEACON HILL *P3*
BLACKHALL ROCKS *P5*
DALTON TOWER *O3*
DALTON-LE-DALE CHURCH *O3*
SEAHAM HARBOUR *O2*

**NORTHERN COUNTY
DURHAM:**
CHESTER-LE-STREET *L2*
LAMBTON CASTLE *M2*
BEAMISH *K2*
CAUSEY ARCH *K2*
TANFIELD RAILWAY *K2*
SHOTLEY BRIDGE SWORDMAKERS *J1*
DERWENTCOTE STEEL FURNACE *J1*
HEDLEY HILL COKE OVENS *J3*
HOWNSGILL VIADUCT *H3*
THOMAS RAW, HIGHWAYMAN *H3*

LANCHESTER ROMAN FORT *J3*
LANGLEY HALL *K3*
MUGGLESWICK GRANGE *H4*
WASKERLEY AND DERWENT RAILWAY *H4*

**WESTERN COUNTY
DURHAM: WEARDALE**
AUCKLAND PALACE *K7*
ST ANDREW'S CHURCH, BISHOP AUCK-
LAND *K6*
NEWTON CAP VIADUCT *K6*
BINCHESTER ROMAN FORT *K6*
ESCOMB CHURCH *J7*
DEVIL'S STONES, CROOK *J5*
JOHN DUCKET MEMORIAL *I4*
WHITFIELD HOUSE *H5*
WHITE KIRKLEY LIME KILNS *G4*
ST THOMAS' CHURCH, STANHOPE *F4*
STANHOPE POLICE STATION AND
COURTHOUSE *F4*
STANHOPE OLD HALL *F4*
HEATHERY BURN CAVE *F3*
CRAWLEYSIDE CABLE RAILWAY *F3*
ROOKHOPE SMELT MILL *E3*
BOLTS LAW INCLINE *F3*
WESTERNHOPEBURN FARM *E4*
HIGH MILL *E4*
WESLEY'S TREE *E4*
WEST BLACKDENE *D4*
BURNHOPE RESERVOIR *D5*

**WESTERN COUNTY
DURHAM: TEESDALE**
COCKFIELD *I7*
SKEW BRIDGE *I7*
COPLEY CHIMNEY *I7*
THE CASTLES, HAMSTERLEY *H6*
RABY CASTLE *I8*
WINSTON BRIDGE *K10*
THE CASTLE, BARNARD CASTLE *H10*
BARNARD CASTLE BRIDGE *H10*
BARNARD CASTLE MARKET CROSS *G10*
BOWES MUSEUM *H10*
EGGLESTONE ABBEY *H10*
ROKEBY HOUSE *J10*
GRETA BRIDGE *J10*
ST GILES' CHURCH *F11*
BOWES CASTLE *F11*
THE BUTTERSTONE, COTHERSTONE *F11*
ROMALDKIRK *G8*
KIRKCARRION *E9*
EGGLESTONE BURIAL MOUND *F8*
COUNTY BRIDGE, MIDDLETON-IN-
TEESDALE *E8*
ST MARY'S CHURCH, MIDDLETON-IN-
TEESDALE *E8*

SEDLING RAKE MINE *D4*
KILLHOPE LEAD MINING CENTRE *D4*
EDMUNDBYERS *G3*
SWINHOPE HEAD HOUSE *E6*

COLDBERRY LEAD MINES *E7*
SKEARS HUSHES *E7*
NEWBIGGIN CHAPEL *D8*
WYNCH BRIDGE *C7*
GIBSON'S CAVE *C7*
CARR CRAGS *D6*

**SOUTHERN COUNTY
DURHAM:**
WESTERTON TOWER *L6*
HETT VILLAGE *L5*
HARDWICK HALL GATE HOUSE *N7*
BISHOP MIDDLEHAM PARK WALL *N6*
FERRYHILL WINDMILL *L6*
CLEVES CROSS, FERRYHILL *L6*
BISHOPTON CASTLE *N7*
WALWORTH CASTLE *N9*
OVINGTON, MAYPOLE VILLAGE *J11*
GAINFORD SPA *K10*
HIGH CONISCLIFFE CHURCH *L10*
PIERCEBRIDGE *L10*
SADBERGE *N10*
TIMOTHY HACKWORTH MUSEUM *L8*
LOCOMOTION AND THE STOCKTON
AND DARLINGTON RAILWAY *M9*
EMERSON, MATHEMATICIAN *M11*
HELL KETTLES *L11*
SOCKBURN AND THE WORM *N12*

Acknowledgements

The authors express their grateful thanks to the following people for their help and co-operation in the preparation of this book: Revd Robert Cooper, Jill Cheesmond, Anne Dunlop, Bill Fawcett, Alex Fitzsimmons and the Durham Dales Mining Society, Rob George, Niall Hammond, Monica Marshall, Tommy Mothersill, Donald Miller, Roger Norris, Sophy Nixon, Mark Nixon, Valerie Nixon, Jim Potts, Beryl Purvis, Colin Rutherford, David Sherlock of English Heritage, Margaret Statham, Ella and Angela Steel, John Wearmouth, Stuart Watt, Don Wilcock, Carol Attewell and the staff at Belmont Library, Judith Crow and the staff at Stanhope Tourist Information Centre, Bill Nixon, Anna H.Bell, Gwen Wilkinson, Anton Rippon at Breedon Books, Ian Forbes, Brian Poole.

Particular thanks are due to Don Wilcock, whose help with industrial archaeology and the history of railways is much appreciated, especially concerning Belmont Viaduct, Copley Chimney, Hedley Hill Coke Ovens, Hownsgill Viaduct and Skew Bridge.

Durham City

Durham Cathedral

DURHAM Cathedral is regarded as the most beautiful religious building in the world. It also enjoys a magnificent setting, high on a sylvan-fringed peninsula formed by a loop in the River Wear. Together with the nearby Durham Castle and the surrounding buildings it was designated a World Heritage Site by UNESCO (United Nations Educational, Scientific and Cultural Organisation) on 28 November 1986. It is a most impressive building, one of the finest examples of Norman architecture anywhere in the world. It stands over the city like a brooding, immortal, monumental matriarch.

Durham Cathedral and the River Wear.

To understand the beginning of the cathedral we have to go back to the time of the Battle of Heavenfield in 634 AD, when King Oswald of Northumbria defeated the pagan hordes of Cadwallon to re-establish Christianity in Northumbria. He sent to Iona for a missionary but the first monk who arrived was said to be beaten by the intractable nature of the people he had come to teach. Then the wise and gentle Aidan arrived and he successfully established a monastery on Lindisfarne. From this humble beginning the importance of this small island grew, and as the Christian word was spread far and wide, it came to be known as 'the Cradle of Christianity'. At the time of the Battle of Heavenfield a boy was born in the Border hills who was des-

Prebends' Bridge (left) and the Cathedral Cloisters (right).

tined to play a major part in the spread of Christianity, and also in the founding of Durham City.

His name was Cuthbert. When he was a young man tending sheep in the Border hills he had a vision of a saint's body being carried up to Heaven by a Heavenly Host of Angels. He later learned that this was the body of Aidan and, profoundly moved by what he had seen, set off to join the religious community at Melrose. He went on to be a highly-respected religious leader and eventually became Bishop of Lindisfarne, after spending ten years as a hermit on Inner Farne, the largest of the Farne Islands. Cuthbert died on Inner Farne on 20 March 687 AD and was buried in the church on Lindisfarne. On his deathbed he warned his brethren that should the need arise they should take his body from the grave rather than it be subject to the control of heathens. Eleven years after his death a miracle was discovered which incontestably proved his saintliness — the coffin was opened so that his body could be venerated and it was found to be incorrupt.

The monks of Lindisfarne, overjoyed, and perhaps a little frightened, placed his body in a new coffin which would eventually become the very essence of the foundation of Durham Cathedral.

In 875 AD the fierce Vikings were raiding the Northumbrian coast, plundering the riches of the monasteries. During one particularly barbarous raid on Lindisfarne, the monks fled and, remembering his deathbed warning, took St Cuthbert's coffin with them.

It was an elaborately carved oak casket with two interior sections. In the lower was St Cuthbert's incorrupt body together with the bones of St Aidan, the bones of Eata of Melrose, and the head of St Oswald. The upper section held the valuable Lindisfarne Gospels and other illuminated manuscripts and treasures. Their wanderings eventually led the party to Chester-le-Street where the saint's body rested for 113 years until, once more in fear of the Viking raiders, the monks fled, this time to Ripon where they stayed for a while with the religious community until the danger had passed, before returning north again.

In 995 AD they were prevented from reaching Chester-le-Street by the wish of their saint, expressed in a vision. They stopped at Durham, or Dunholme, the hill island. Here, under the leadership of their Saxon bishop, Alduhn, they constructed a temporary

The Rose Window

(opposite page) Durham Cathedral, the Fulling Mill and the River Wear.

shelter of boughs to protect the coffin. This was soon replaced by a more permanent wooden church, but even this wasn't to last. On 4 September 998 a stone church, known as the 'White Church', was dedicated and the saint's body laid within its precincts. Up to the Conquest this church was served by secular priests. They had wives and families who lived in homes separate from the church. This 'Congregation of St Cuthbert', was to be ejected by the first Norman bishop, Walcher of Lorraine (1071-80), but before he could carry out this change he was murdered by a mob at Gateshead.

William the Conqueror's response to this was 'The Harrying of the North' and by 1081 he and his soldiers had totally devastated the area.

Bishop William de St Carileph was given charge over the secular community at Durham and it was he who ultimately ejected them, replacing them with his Benedictine monks from the newly-formed communities of Jarrow and Wearmouth, who were to occupy the cathedral until the Reformation. After several years exile in France, as a result of being wrongly accused of plotting against the King, the Bishop returned to Durham and ordered the construction of the Cathedral to

begin. On 11 August 1093 the foundation stone was laid. Unfortunately, William de St Carileph did not live to see Durham Cathedral completed, for he died in 1132.

In the following centuries various bishops all added their own contributions to the cathedral. Bishop Hugh Pudsey, for instance, made several major alterations during the 12th century and in 1175 he added the Galilee Chapel to the west end. This chapel is now the resting place for another important ecclesiastical figure, the Venerable Bede — the 'Father of English History' and the author of the original *Life of St Cuthbert.*

Although Durham Cathedral is renowned for its Norman architecture it also has excellent examples from other periods and both Geometrical and Perpendicular styles are well represented. The Romanesque pillars of the nave are particularly impressive and with their characteristic bold decorative style they form a perfect geometric pattern leading to the magnificent Rose Window, high above the Chapel of the Nine Altars. The roof of the nave is rib-vaulted, the earliest example in any cathedral. The pillars of the Chapel of the Nine Altars are in our own county's Frosterley marble, a fossilised carboniferous limestone, once highly valued for decorative building purposes, all over the world. The choir stalls are a fine example of Bishop John Cosin's Restoration woodwork. The 4,000 Scottish prisoners held in Durham Cathedral by Oliver Cromwell in 1650 were responsible for destroying much of its earlier woodwork. They also severely damaged the Neville tomb — revenge, perhaps for that family's military prowess in the Border Wars. Above the

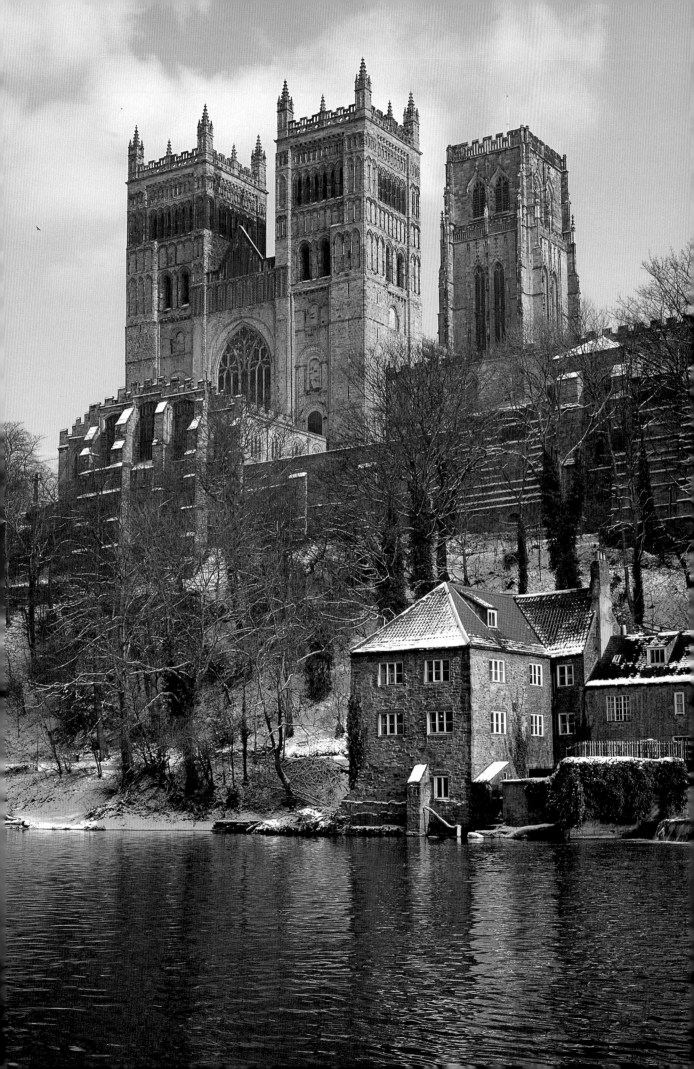

tomb of Bishop Hatfield is the Bishop's throne, or 'cathedra', the highest in Christendom, an indication of the status of the Bishop of Durham. Behind the magnificent Neville Screen of Caen stone is the tomb of St Cuthbert. The coffin has lain beneath this simple marble slab bearing the inscription 'Cuthbertus', since 1104. This became the focal point of Christianity in the north and many thousands of pilgrims made great journeys to worship here.

Across the western end of the cathedral, by the font, is a line of Frosterley marble set into the floor. Originally the West Door was the main entrance and women could not cross beyond this line further into the church because of St Cuthbert's supposed hatred of females.

According to the 19th-century historian and traveller John Murray, *'This is attributed to a false charge of seduction made against him by a daughter of one of the Pictish kings'*. To allow women to worship, Bishop Pudsey built the Galilee Chapel. In spite of this legend we are told by Bede that St Cuthbert had many women friends, whom he held in high regard.

The Monks' Dormitory dates from 1400 and houses a fine collection of Anglo-Saxon carved stonework and many wonderful books with illuminated manuscript.

The cloister was the very centre of the monks' daily life. Its building was begun in 1368 at the order of Bishop Skirlaw but not finished until 1498, during the reign of Bishop Langley — longer than it took to build the cathedral.

Naturally Durham Cathedral has always been regarded with special affec-

tion by the people of Durham and, indeed, St Cuthbert is said to give special protection to the building and the people of the city. One of the more recent examples occurred during World War Two on 1 May 1942, at about 2.40am.

Gwen Wilkinson, a resident of South Street, which is set high on the river bank opposite the western towers of the cathedral, was on fire-watching duty when the sirens wailed their eerie sound echoing across the river in the early hours. Durham was to be the target of a bombing raid as revenge for the escalating heavy raids on Germany. In fact, this had been broadcast by 'Lord Haw Haw' only a few days previously. As Gwen stepped out of the house she was greeted with the unforgettable sight of the cathedral, castle and river banks bathed in brilliant silver moonlight. Suddenly, a mist began to rise from the river far below. It soon blotted out the scene, swirling up around the central and two western towers of the cathedral. A cloud covered the moon and the whole area was transformed, shrouded in a dark, dense mist. She heard the sound of enemy planes passing overhead. They circled but were unable to locate their target and withdrew. The all-clear sounded and Gwen returned home. As she closed her front door she removed her tin helmet and stood in silence with her head bowed, to thank God for deliverance. She was convinced that Saint Cuthbert had protected his city.

Many wonderful stories and legends abound about this magnificent building, and the man in whose honour it was built. It will always stand as the symbol and the shrine to this humble pioneer of Christianity in the north.

Bedesmen's Bench, Durham Cathedral

SET into the north wall of the North Choir of Durham Cathedral, opposite the tomb of Bishop Skirlaw, is a stone bench with the bishop's shield carved on alternate panels. This is the Bedesmen's Bench. The name 'bedesman', or 'beadsman', as it is sometimes spelt, means 'a man of prayer' and is derived from the Old English word 'biddan', which means 'to pray'. These men would be paid to pray for others and would sit on the bench waiting for a benefactor.

The bedesmen were formed by Walter Skirlaw who was Bishop of Durham from 1388 to 1405. Although they are not unique to Durham, bedesmen are an unusual part of the Cathedral Foundation. A few other cathedrals do have them, but only Durham retains its full complement of eight. The bedesmen are chosen from men who have served with credit in Her Majesty's Forces and up until the 1920s it was a Crown appointment, although now it is the responsibility of the Dean and Chapter.

The position is an ancient one and the Statutes of the Cathedral from 10 March 1555, under which the Cathedral Foundation was renewed after the dissolution of the Priory, state that: *'There shall be eight poor men to be nourished out of the goods of the church, men oppressed with poverty and distressed by want, or crippled and mutilated in warfare, or worn out with old age, or in some other way reduced to weakness and want.'*

The statutes go on to say that these men should also help the sub-sacrists with the lighting and the putting out of

Bedesmen's Bench.

the lights and ringing the bells, plus any other duties the dean may require.

Today the bedesmen mainly look after the western end of the cathedral and assist the vergers in its day-to-day running, and indeed, its preparation for services. When they are not performing these duties they answer questions and supply information for visitors.

Thankfully, though, these days they are neither oppressed or distressed, except perhaps at the height of the tourist season!

Dun Cow Panel, Durham Cathedral

A PANEL on the north-west turret of the Chapel of the Nine Altars of Durham Cathedral commemorates the legend of the Dun Cow and of how St Cuthbert's body came to be enshrined at Durham.

Cuthbert died in 687 AD on Inner Farne and was buried in the church on Lindisfarne. On his deathbed he had spoken to his fellow monks of moving his body if ever it became necessary. Just over 200 years later the necessity arose when the Vikings repeatedly raided Northumbria, plundering, pillaging, raping, killing and laying waste the land. The monks of Lindisfarne took the body of St Cuthbert and fled in the face of this privation and danger, to wander for seven long years among the ruined churches and monasteries of Northumbria.

Eventually the party arrived in Chester-le-Street, an old Roman station, where they built a shrine for the coffin. They settled here for over 100 years. Then once more the Vikings raided Northumbria and Bishop Alduhn and his monks took the body of St Cuthbert and moved south to Ripon. A few months later, when peace was restored, the party set off to return home with the body of their beloved saint.

They had reached 'Wrdelau', a place just to the east of what is now

Dun Cow panel.

Durham City, when the procession came to an unscheduled halt. Legend has it that the bier on which the coffin was being carried became fixed and no amount of effort could persuade it to move. The saint obviously did not wish to return to Chester-le-Street, but the monks had no idea where to take him. For three days they fasted and prayed and then, St Cuthbert appeared in a vision and told one of the brethren, Eadmer, that they must take his body to 'Dunholme' — the Hill Island. But where was Dunholme? The monks were deeply distressed because none of them knew. Then, as fortune would have it, one of the brethren heard two dairymaids talking. One of them had lost a cow and she was told it had wandered on to the Dunholme. The monks were overjoyed and guided by the girl they moved the coffin to the naturally defendable peninsula where they set it down and constructed a rough shelter of boughs to protect the precious burden they had carried for so long. They had found the final resting place for St Cuthbert.

The sculpture on the chapel turret depicting the legend is a 1779 restoration by George Nicholson, the builder of Prebends' Bridge. It is described as '*restored and finished with much art*' by Hutchinson. However, it bears only a remote resemblance to the original and this has caused much dissatisfaction with several other historians.

Some people are inclined to explain away the story of the Dun Cow as a reflection based on an old proverb about the wealth of later Durham — '*The Dun Cow's milk makes the Prebends' wives go all in silk*'. The earliest documentation of the legend dates from the 16th century, but, whatever the truth, it lends a certain degree of romantic mysticism to the wonderful story of St Cuthbert.

The Sanctuary Knocker, Durham Cathedral

DURING the Middle Ages every church afforded temporary sanctuary to people fleeing from the pursuit of the avenger, but these privileges were extra special in churches where the relics of saints rested. Durham Cathedral was one such place, the right of sanctuary being closely associated with the body of St Cuthbert. A hunted criminal would be safe from the hue and cry once he had grasped the ring of the Sanctuary Knocker. At that time there were two chambers over the North Door which were occupied by the monks whose duty it was to admit those persons seeking sanctuary. Once the scoundrel had been admitted, the Galilee Bell would be rung and his confession heard. His details would then be carefully recorded in the Sanctuary Book.

The original book, which is still in the cathedral, was kept from 1464 to 1525 and lists 331 criminals. The entries are mainly in Latin and give the name and place of abode of the claimant, the date and place of his crime and the name of the victim plus any other relevant particulars. Each entry closes with the names of the witnesses who heard the criminal's confession. Of the 331 entries, 283 are murderers and the rest an assortment of horse thieves, cattle rustlers, prison breakers, burglars and debtors. Men on the run came from all over the north; Newcastle in particular is mentioned eight times.

Once the felon was inside he had to wear a simple gown of black cloth with a yellow St Cuthbert's cross on the shoulder so that everyone knew he was enjoying the privilege of sanctuary.

He could remain in safety for 37 days. After that, if his pursuers were persistent, or no Royal Pardon was forthcoming, he would have to set out, bare-headed and in his distinctive costume, carrying only a simple wooden cross, for the coast to board a ship and leave the country. He had to keep to the King's highway and could not remain in one place for more than two nights. The time limit allowed, necessitated a tight schedule. For instance, one man was given only nine days to walk to Dover. In practice, however, communication was so bad between different parts of the country, as often as not the criminal would proceed a discreet distance and then begin a new life as a seemingly respectable citizen.

The privilege of sanctuary was born of the belief that the church was holy and that anyone who touched the church or its precincts became 'infected' with its holiness. Durham Cathedral possessed 'peculiar sanctuary', whereby immunity could be granted for serious crimes, even high treason. The only crime which could not, or

The Sanctuary Knocker, the North Door, Durham Cathedral.

indeed, would not be forgiven was sacrilege.

The right of sanctuary was often abused but it was rigorously claimed by the church right up to the Reformation.

The Sanctuary Knocker seen on the North Door today is a copy of the original, which is now on display in the Cathedral. The original would perhaps have had enamelled eyes where there are now only empty sockets, which, nevertheless, add to its sinister charm.

Durham Castle, University College

THERE are few castles in England as well situated as Durham Castle, and there are none with such an impressive neighbour as Durham Cathedral.

Long before the Norman invasion the monks of Lindisfarne had erected fortifications on this naturally defensible spot to afford extra protection for the Shrine of St Cuthbert. This was so effective it repelled attacks mounted by the armies of two kings of Scotland, Duncan and Malcolm III.

In 1072 William the Conqueror stayed in Durham when he broke his journey northwards, to Scotland. He was so impressed with the site that he gave orders for a castle to be built; and it would remain uncaptured during the following 400 years of border warfare.

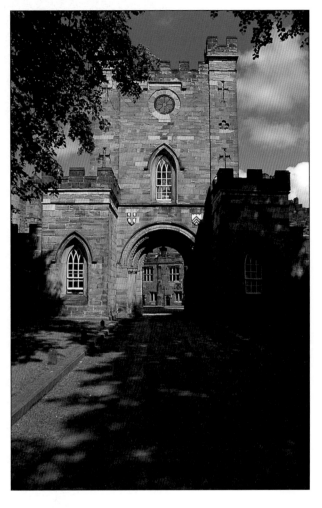

The Castle Gate-house (left). Bishop John Cosin's Coat of Arms (right).

The earliest parts of the castle were built by Waltheof, Earl of Northumberland, although within the space of a few years the King had granted custody of the new stronghold to the ill-fated first Norman Prince Bishop, Walcher of Lorraine, who added several architectural improvements of his own as did his successor, William de St Carileph. Ralph Flambard, Bishop from 1099 to 1128, also made a large contribution to the early building.

Hugh Pudsey made many additions and alterations in the century after its foundation. Anthony Bek contributed the Great Hall in the 13th century and Thomas Hatfield added the Keep in the 14th century. Bishop Richard Fox converted the guardroom into the kitchen, which is still in use today.

Cuthbert Tunstall was bishop at the Dissolution and it was he who achieved a more residential aspect for the castle, also adding the chapel which was extended by Nathaniel, Lord Crewe, in 1700, and which is also still in use today.

John Cosin was the first bishop after the Restoration and he found the castle in a ruinous state. He spent a vast amount of money restoring the building to its former glory, the famous Black Oak Staircase being one of his many additions.

The gatehouse was built on the earlier Norman foundations in 1800 for Bishop Shute Barrington by James Wyatt, a notorious architect whose reputation causes much controversy among historians and lovers of architecture.

Further restoration and improvements were carried out right up until 1837, when William van Mildert, the

(opposite page) The Castle and Brown's boathouse.

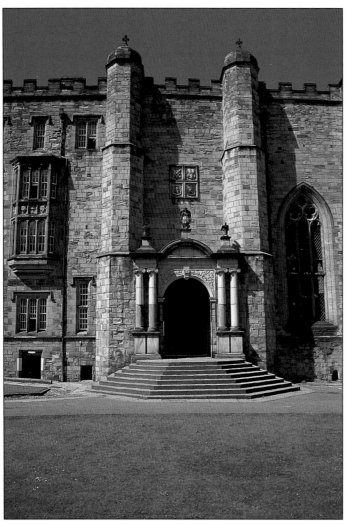

Main entrance of Durham Castle.

For almost 800 years Durham Castle was the home of the powerful Prince Bishops. Today, no less a distinction, it is University College for the third oldest university in England, and it is most certainly Britain's oldest and most romantic university hall of residence.

The Londonderry Statue

DURHAM'S citizens hurrying about their daily business have little time to glance up at their distinctive equestrian statue, familiarly referred to as 'The Man On The Horse In The Market Place'. Fortunately it is usually admired by Durham's visitors, although often without realising its true significance in history. It commemorates the remarkable life of the 3rd Marquess of Londonderry (1778-1854) and is modelled upon him as a dashing hussar on his powerful charger. The Marchioness commissioned it, along with other memorials to her distinguished husband, and presented it to the city.

last Prince Bishop, gave the castle to Durham University, which he had helped establish, five years earlier.

Durham Castle is a typical motte and bailey stronghold, with its keep on one side of a courtyard, enclosed by buildings along the other two sides — a most effective defence.

The Keep, Durham Castle.

Charles William Stewart was of noble birth, educated at Eton, and was soon to gain a reputation as a courageous cavalry officer. He sat in the old Irish Parliament, as well as at Westminster, from 1801 until 1814. He rose to the rank of major-general before being invalided out of the Peninsular War, where he had served with distinction under Sir Arthur Wellesley, who was to become the Duke of Wellington. Honours were showered upon him and he was raised to the peerage as Baron Stewart of Stewart's Court and Ballylawn, County Donegal, in advance of being appointed, in 1814, Britain's ambassador to Austria, still then a monarchy. This was before he moved

into the County Durham scene and achieved further accomplishments, such as creating the harbour at Seaham.

Lady Londonderry would have been hard pressed to think of a monument design befitting such high achievement, but she was not daunted. She engaged an Italian sculptor, Raffaelle Monti of Milan, to create her ambition, using a new process of copper plating which had been under development for some time, but never successfully used on such a grand scale. Due to the difficulties encountered, Monti incurred considerable financial outlay and Lady Londonderry was persuaded to pay the sculptor in advance. Upon the eventual completion of the statue, Monti was declared bankrupt and it was seized by his creditors while still in his workshop. In order to retrieve it, Lady Londonderry had to pay a further substantial sum, upon which ultimatum she reacted most vociferously.

There had been some controversy before selecting the site for the monument but further discord was to follow the decision. Upon seeing the substantial stone pedestal rising in the Market Place, five Durham businessmen filed a court petition claiming that it was going to interfere with access to the markets, detract from St Nicholas' Church and damage their businesses. Fortunately the case was rejected and its erection resumed.

Lady Londonderry's pride at witnessing the unveiling ceremony on 2 December 1861 must have been somewhat dampened by memories of these unfortunate developments but she would be amply comforted by having her life-long friend, the Prime Minister, Benjamin Disraeli, at her side, both then and afterwards at the celebratory luncheon when he spoke most affectionately of his friend, the 3rd Marquess of Londonderry.

The Londonderry Statue, Market Place.

North Road Drinking Fountain

ERECTED by public subscription in 1863, originally on a site between the railway viaduct as it crosses above North Road and the then corner of Atherton Street, this impressively designed drinking fountain is now removed to the foot of another viaduct pier where, despite its substantial dimensions, it is dwarfed by this massive engineering feat.

North Road Drinking Fountain.

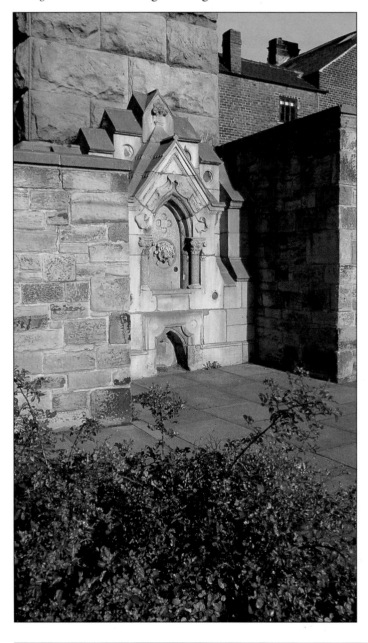

Designed in Gothic style, principally using Dunhouse stone, it is further embellished with Peterhead Red granite columns and Rubislaw Grey granite centre panel. The source of the water supply was the Flass Well at the foot of Redhill which was piped here to two gargoyles, serving first the marble drinking bowl and passing on to the dog trough below.

Sadly no longer functioning, the 'fountain' now only serves as an interesting example of street furniture, no longer appreciated.

House of Correction, Elvet Bridge

IN 1632 the House of Correction was built into the northern arches of Bishop Pudsey's 12th-century Elvet Bridge, on the site of the chantry of St James. It remained in use until 1819, when its inmates were transferred to the new goal at the head of Elvet, and it stood empty until it was sold by auction in 1821. Its distinction from the North Gate County Goal, built by Bishop Langley in the early 15th century, is said to be that it was used for lunatics, vagrants and those awaiting trial. Its most renowned inhabitant was Jamie Allan, but he was there for a different reason.

He was born of gypsy parentage near Rothbury in the 1730s and his accomplishment on the Northumbrian pipes earned him recognition by the Duchess of Northumberland. He became resident at Alnwick but soon misbehaved and lost her favour. Subsequently he led a remarkable and irresponsible itinerant life throughout Europe, Asia and Africa

House of Correction, Elvet Bridge.

this last journey was not enforced and he spent the remaining seven years of his life in the House of Correction.

He died in 1810 on the day before the Prince Regent granted him a free pardon. It is said that his ghost wanders the dank, dark cells and that the plaintive sound of his pipes can sometimes be heard.

No wonder! What greater punishment to a wandering gypsy than this? Even his request to be buried in his native Rothbury went unheeded and he was interred in St Nicholas' Churchyard, now part of Durham's busy Market Place.

but on his return was convicted, in 1803 at Durham Assizes, of horse stealing and condemned to death. This sentence was later commuted to transportation but, probably due to his advanced age and poor health,

The Watergate, South Bailey

THE Watergate was erected in 1778 to replace the old postern gate in the city wall which gave exit from the city and guarded the river crossing.

The Watergate.

The Revd Henry Egerton bought the postern gate and the adjoining property, demolished it and replaced it with this simple, graceful arch, high enough to allow carriages to approach the newly-built Prebends' Bridge which had succeeded the horse and foot bridge of 1574, swept away in the Great Flood of 1771.

This is a good location from which to observe the remains of the rugged City walls. Many visitors overlook this interesting feature as they are either intrigued by the curving range of architectural phases in the South Bailey or drawn towards the splendour of Prebends' Bridge.

The Revd Henry Egerton, a prebendary of Durham, was brother of the Bishop, John Egerton, 1771-87. He was renowned for his good works for the poor of the city and died in 1793. He lies in St Giles' Churchyard.

Shipperdson's Cottage, river banks.

Shipperdson's Cottage

NESTLING in an idyllic position on Durham City's river banks, is an attractive garden retreat, built in the 1820s to serve Mr Shipperdson, who owned the property in South Bailey which towers above the steep, wooded hillside. Since then, residents and visitors have admired this most distinctive landmark.

It has been misleadingly referred to as the 'Count's House', although the nearby actual home of Polish Count Jozef Boruwlaski was demolished after his death. It has also been variously described as a folly, a gardener's cottage and a garden house.

Count Boruwlaski was born in Poland in 1739 but spent the last 15 years of his remarkably long life in Durham, dying at the age of 97. He was an intellectual and an accomplished

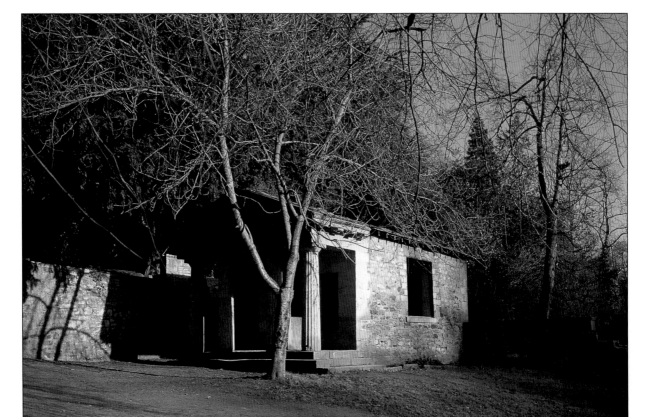

musician and he enjoyed the confidences of royalty and nobility, yet he was an unfortunate man, sometimes humiliated. He was a dwarf, only 3ft 3ins high, although perfectly proportioned, and he used to claim he was normal in every way except in size. Born of normal-sized parents he was one of six children. However, his elder brother and young sister were also dwarfs. He was orphaned when only nine years old but enjoyed good health, as his eventual great age confirmed. He married a lady of his own nationality and all three of his children were of normal size.

Rarely do dwarfs achieve such an age and he eventually qualified for inclusion in the *Guinness Book Of Records.* He was indeed a remarkable man and is buried in the Cathedral, under the North Western Tower, although his memorial tablet is erected in the nave of St Mary-the-less in the South Bailey.

Perhaps his autograph could also be his epitaph. He used to write:

> *'Poland was my cradle*
> *England is my nest*
> *Durham is my quiet place*
> *Where my bones will rest'*

Banksman's Cottage

THE Banksman's Cottage has long been otherwise known as either Prebends' Bridge Cottage, Prebends' Cottage, or Betsy's Cottage. When it was originally built, sometime before 1820 and probably contemporary with Prebends' Bridge from the 1770s, it was the attractively designed and situated dwelling of the Banksman to the Dean and Chapter.

He was responsible for keeping the river banks and paths clean, orderly and safe from obstructions. It was he whom we could thank for the repetitive thud of the axe clearing the fallen

Banksman's Cottage, the river banks.

boughs; for the blue smoke spiralling skywards or drifting towards us with that unmistakeable and evocative scent, inducing a certain comfort to an enjoyable riverside walk.

His cottage is now let to University students who possibly have the most charming accommodation in Durham.

South Street Mill

THE Corn Mill on the river banks below Durham's South Street is of uncertain date, and was not recorded in the *Boldon Book* of 1185, like Bishop's Mill, further downstream. The mill does seem to have existed before Scaltok Mill was abandoned, when the River Wear changed course at Hollow Drift in the 15th century, leaving it without power.

South Street Mill.

Like the Fulling Mill on the opposite river bank, now the Museum of Archaeology, it too belonged to the Priory which seems to have had the monopoly of mills on the Wear at Durham, although the Bishop owned the mill below Milburngate Bridge and Kepier Hospital owned another further downstream. Kepier Mill burned down in 1870 and has virtually disappeared. Only the millrace arch is left to indicate its location.

South Street Mill would serve all those tenants of the Priory lands in the Barony of Elvet. They were enforced to bring their corn to the landlord's mill, as a condition of tenancy. Comprising two mills, it must once have presented a busy scene, but now in its seclusion it makes an attractive and romantic contribution to the sylvan river banks of Durham City.

Charley Cross, Church Street Head

NOW re-sited within iron railings behind the hedge-line where Church Street curves into Quarryheads Lane, this rugged stone stump, set in a chamfered stone base, is all that survives of this possibly

13th-century wayside cross which is reputed to have stood on a triple base in the middle of these crossroads. It was moved to the grounds of Bow School, but post-war road widening required its further re-siting in Palmers' Close.

This cross could have served a dual role as a monastic boundary stone. Palmers' Close was granted to the monastery by Prior Bertram's nephew and was used by pilgrims (or palmers) to graze their horses while they wor-shipped at St Cuthbert's shrine. Pilgrims would descend the steep path to cross the river below, by the ford in the early days, and later by using the foot-bridge which pre-dated Prebends' Bridge. They would enter the city by the Watergate and walk along the Bailey towards the cathedral.

Charley Cross.

Durham Light Infantry Museum

THIS museum traces the history of County Durham's own regiment from its early history in 1758 to when it was disbanded in 1968. The regiment's individual identity disappeared as the Durham Light Infantry when it merged with three other regiments to become simply known as 'The Light Infantry'. The 'Faithfuls', as they were known, have seen action all over the world. In

Durham Light Infantry Memorial Garden, Durham Cathedral.

Trench reconstruction (left). Adam Wakenshaw's anti-tank gun (right).

the West Indies thousands of men died of rampant disease and it was during those days that the regimental motto 'Faithful' was adopted.

In the Peninsular War, in 1811, they fought under Sir Arthur Wellesley — the Duke Of Wellington — against Napoleon, winning their first battle honours. They also saw action in the Indian Mutiny under the East India Company. During the Crimean War, in 1854, the regiment was in battle at Alma, Balaclava, Inkerman, and the siege of Sebastopol. Two of the soldiers in this war, John Byrne and Thomas de Courcey, were awarded the newly-created Victoria Cross. Some of the troops who had fought in the Crimea also fought in New Zealand, helping the European settlers

defeat the warring Maoris. In the final battle, at Te Ranga, another Victoria Cross was awarded, to John Murray.

The Boer War in South Africa from 1899-1902 saw the regiment in action again, fighting at Colenso, Spion Kop, Vaal Krantz and in the relief of Ladysmith — and again the soldiers of the DLI distinguished themselves.

In World War One, from 1914-18, the regiment was in the thick of the action again, but suffered heavy casualties. They fought in every major battle in the war, all of them etched on history as bloody conflicts — Ypres, Arras, Messines, the Somme and Passchendaele. The regiment was awarded six Victoria Crosses, but at great cost — almost 13,000 men were killed and

Armoured personnel carrier (left) and The Durham Light Infantry's Regimental Badge (right).

thousands more were gassed, wounded, or taken prisoner.

In World War Two, from 1939-45, eight battalions of the Durham Light Infantry saw action, and fought with distinction in every theatre of war — Dunkirk, North Africa, Malta, Sicily, Italy and Burma. In

Europe they fought from D-Day on 6 June 1944 right up to the Nazi surrender on 7 May 1945. Two Victoria Crosses were won by DLI soldiers in World War Two. They were by Captain Richard Annand, in Belgium, for preventing the attack on a bridge and rescuing his wounded batman by pushing him to safety in a wheelbarrow, and, posthumously, by Adam Wakenshaw at Mersa Matruh in North Africa, for continuing to man his anti-tank gun under heavy attack, even though he was mortally wounded. The regiment went on to fight as part of the United Nations forces in Korea from 1952 to 1953 and they later served in Cyprus and Berlin. Their last campaign was in the swamps and jungles of Borneo, in 1966.

On 12 December 1968 the Durham Light Infantry paraded its colours for the last time, fittingly in Durham Cathedral. There is a chapel with remembrance book, dedicated to the Regiment, in the cathedral and also a memorial garden.

The museum contains much of interest, such as uniforms, weapons and vehicles. There is also a medal room displaying some of the honours won by the soldiers on active service, fitting reminders of the history of this remarkable local regiment.

The Battle of Nevilles Cross

DURING the Middle Ages the border area of England and Scotland was in constant turmoil. Many battles were fought between the two countries. The fact that the Scots enjoyed the support of the French, who were also at variance with the English over the possession of lands in France, only served to compound the problem. The Battle of Nevilles Cross, which took place just to the west of Durham City, was perhaps one of the more important border battles, although it was, in fact, the culmination of a series of events. The English, under the command of Edward III, defeated the French army, under the command of Philip VI, at the Battle of Crecy in August 1346. They then marched on Calais and held it under siege. To seek relief from the situation, Philip asked David II of Scotland to create a diversion by mounting an invasion of northern England.

By the beginning of October, King David had raised an army and crossed the border just north of Carlisle. The Scots forged along the Tyne valley, sacking Lanercost Priory and taking Hexham and neighbouring Corbridge. They crossed the Tyne at the ford

The Battle of Nevilles Cross monument.

The Battle of Nevilles Cross sculpture at Durham Johnston School.

message to King David warning him to withdraw and return to Scotland but this was ignored. Even the pleading of two monks from Durham failed to persuade the Scots not to fight. The night before the battle St Cuthbert is said to have appeared to the Prior of Durham, John Fossor, instructing him to take the saint's banner to the battlefield. It was taken to Maiden's Bower where a group of monks spent the duration of the battle in prayer.

The battle was fought on 17 October 1346. The English army, of about 5,000 men, had advanced to form at Crossgate Moor. The Scottish army, with possibly 16,000 soldiers, advanced from Beaurepaire and drew up a little to the north. A bloody battle ensued and the Scots were defeated.

The Scottish King's standard bearer, Alexander Ramsay, was killed and David himself was wounded by arrows. He was captured by John Copeland: one story is that the King's reflection in the water under Aldin Grange Bridge, where he was hiding, gave him away. The other story is that, despite being wounded, King David put up a staunch struggle against his determined captor.

King David was taken to a Northumbrian castle to recover from his wounds and afterwards was held prisoner in the Tower of London for 11 years. He was eventually ransomed for £66,000 — the equivalent of £15 million in present values — a king's ransom indeed.

The Nevilles were one of the most powerful and influential families in England during the Middle Ages. After the battle, Sir Ralph Neville erected a cross at the site to honour his great vic-

between Newburn and Ryton and continued south. Legend has it that just before crossing the River Derwent into Durham, King David had a vision warning him not to invade the lands of St Cuthbert. This went unheeded and the King and his army crossed the river at Ebchester and on 16 October they camped at Beaurepaire (Bearpark) only two miles from Durham City.

Meanwhile, the English army had gathered under the command of Ralph Neville, Henry Percy and the Archbishop of York at Richmond. They advanced to Barnard Castle and on to Bishop Auckland where they camped in Auckland Park, also on 16 October.

At Merrington, mounted English soldiers ran into a Scottish foraging party under the command of William Douglas. The Scots were put to flight and in the running battle which followed many were killed. This area, just to the north of Ferryhill, is still known as 'Butcher Race'. Henry Percy sent a tory. Although it was largely destroyed in the 16th century, part of it can still be seen almost at the very spot where the English army assembled. A local story says that if you walk three times around the cross and put your ear to the ground you can hear the sound of the clash of arms. Sir Ralph's distinction in the battle was such that he was granted the honour of being the first layman to be allowed burial in Durham Cathedral.

Henceforth the banner of St Cuthbert was held in such great esteem and carried such deep significance for the people of the bishopric, that the Earl of Surrey, commander of the English at the Battle of Flodden Field in 1513, asked for it to be carried into battle by the troops from Durham, a further reminder of the powerful influence of this charismatic northern saint.

As part of the 650th commemoration events, a new sculpture was erected in 1996 and can be seen at the entrance to Durham Johnston School. This was created by Graeme Hopper, the artist-in-residence, students and staff of the school, and is a fitting reminder of this significant event in English history.

Aldin Grange Bridge

ONE of Durham's oldest bridges is to be found within two miles of the city where the road to Bearpark and Ushaw College crosses the River Browney. Now bypassed by a late 19th-century bridge alongside, it can easily be overlooked. Described by historians since the earliest writings as 'an old and narrow stone bridge of one arch', it was repaired in 1370 at a cost of thirteen shillings and four pence (67p!).

Its supposed claim to fame is based upon a local legend which tells of how

Aldin Grange Bridge, near Bearpark.

King David of Scotland hid beneath it after his defeat at the Battle of Nevilles Cross in 1346, only to be discovered through his reflection in the water. On the basis of contemporary reports of the battle and his capture lending no support to this story, and in the light of King David's commendable character, this legend would seem not to deserve credence.

The bridge takes its name from nearby Aldin Grange, a medieval manor built on the courtyard principle, which after a chequered history of owners, has gradually developed into a small community of private homes. Sufficiently unspoilt on the courtyard elevations, it attracts film producers seeking authentic period sets.

Maiden Castle

MAIDEN Castle Wood is one of Durham's unsolved mysteries and is likely to remain so until further archaeological work is carried out. There can be little doubt that it was occupied in Iron Age and Roman times as is evidenced by their occupation of the Old Durham site, on the opposite bank of the River Wear, 100ft below. Such advantageous height would not have been neglected for either defence or signalling purposes.

It is the remains of the defensive measures, still visible at the western side of this high platform area with its steeply wooded natural defences, which have long attracted the attention of antiquaries. This engineered line of defence took the form of a substantial ditch across the only vulnerable approach, which Fordyce described as 12 paces wide and he presumed it to have been guarded by a drawbridge. It preceded the 9ft-high earthen rampart by an interval of 20 paces. According to Surtees, writing in 1827, remains of masonry were discovered, suggesting that the rampart had been further protected. Surtees drew much of his information from Hutchinson who had surveyed the site earlier, when it was more complete, but even he was unable to date it with certainty.

For the site's greater defence it should not be overlooked that in earlier times, the river followed a course further round the base of the wood, when it swept in a horseshoe around Hollow Drift before continuing on its present-day course.

It seems surprising that this historical site, so accessible and close to the city centre, should pass unnoticed, unappreciated and unexplored.

Maiden Castle, Ancient British earthwork.

Tinklers' Lane, Claypath

TINKLERS' or Tinkers' Lane is a cobbled vennel which ran quite steeply from the top of Claypath down to the riverside and formed the boundary between the parishes of St Nicholas and St Giles.

Stumbling over the centuries-old cobbles, between the high, whitewashed stone walls, which effectively block out the modern world, it is easy to imagine the sound of tinkers repairing pots and pans for the local townspeople. They brought their kitchen utensils here because tinkers were banned from the city streets.

Its original length has been shortened by the Leazes Link Road and it no longer reaches the riverside. Originally it emerged next to Mitchinson's sweet shop, an extension of Woodbine Cottage — another casualty of the through road scheme.

A very primitive public urinal, positioned near the Claypath entrance, has been removed but the cobbled surface survives to confirm the antiquity of this secret lane.

The Chapel of St Mary Magdalene, Gilesgate

ST MARY Magdalene's Chapel, Gilesgate, was once the chapel of a small hospital said to be founded by one Sir John FitzAlexander. The establishment consisted of a priest and 13 brethren and sisters, defined in an ancient deed as '*Men and women who had been well-to-do folkes and in good repute in their early life, and whose wealth has passed away*'. These people were to be taken into the hospital '*without giving anything for their entry*'. These 'Maudeleyans', as they were known, were clothed and fed under the jurisdiction of the Almoner of Durham Cathedral.

Under the regulations the chaplain had to wear a monk's habit, which would be replaced every year, and the brethren and sisters received 'three ells' of russet and canvas for clothes and the sum of fourpence for shoes. They were also supplied with 23½ loaves of white bread a week and broth on three days a week. In 1391 Bishop Walter Skirlaw granted an indulgence to all those who supported this hospital.

Because of the soft nature of the ground on which it was built, the chapel became unsafe and ruinous and had to be entirely rebuilt a few yards away from its original site, between 1449 and 1451.

The new chapel was consecrated on 16 May 1451 and enjoyed all the rights of a parish church even though its parish only covered 23 acres.

After the Dissolution of the Monasteries in 1546 the chapel continued in use as a place of public worship until

Tinklers' Lane, Claypath.

37

The ruin of the Chapel of St Mary Magdalene, Gilesgate.

the end of the 17th century when its fabric had become dangerous and unsafe.

Vane Tempest Hall, Gilesgate

THE Vane Tempest Hall in Gilesgate is the only surviving example of a militia barracks in County Durham. The Durham Militia was formed in 1759 and Lord Vane, Earl of Darlington was colonel of the regiment. The officers were chosen from among the local gentry while the rank and file men were selected by ballot.

In 1853 the Durham Militia was divided into the North Durham Mili-

(opposite page) Vane Tempest Hall, once the Militia Barracks.

tia, based at Gilesgate, and the South Durham Militia, based at Barnard Castle. The North and South Durham Militia became the 3rd and 4th Battalions of the Durham Light Infantry and fought in the Boer War 1899-1902.

By 1884 the barracks had been vacated, as Revd John Tweedy tells us, '*A hospital for small-pox cases was established in the late militia's barracks in Gilesgate.*' However, we learn that in 1893 '*this building was purchased by the Marquess of Londonderry for the headquarters of the 2nd Durham Artillery Volunteers*'.

The hall today serves the area as a busy community centre, although it is reputed to be haunted by the ghost of a

Surviving brick kiln, Kepier Brickworks.

soldier who was executed in the courtyard, for mutiny.

Brick Kiln, Kepier

THE brick kiln at Kepier is the single remaining example of a series that lined the road to Kepier colliery. It is thought to be of a Scottish design not frequently found in this area, the Newcastle type being usually adopted.

Brickmaking was recorded as already established on this site in 1828 when Thomas Jackson, a local builder and stonemason was listed as proprietor. The firm became Thomas Jackson & Son of Claypath in 1834. They were succeeded by Eleanor Jackson in 1848 who was described as a brickmaker and stonemason of the Sands as late as 1857.

By 1860, Kepier brickworks was con-trolled by John Thwaites who succeeded Ralph Dixon as owner of Kepier colliery in 1857, after which it was in the hands of W.Tinker. But it does not seem to have continued in operation much beyond that date.

Kepier Quarries

KEPIER'S long-abandoned quarry faces provide a rugged backdrop for the trees which have naturalised this riverside walk. It is remote from the popular river banks of the city, but much appreciated by those fortunate enough to know this stretch of the river.

The quarries range almost continuously along the length of the woodland and inevitably prompt the question, 'Where has all the stone been used?' It is sandstone, and, unlike limestone, cannot be used for any purpose other than building material. Moreover, most of the stone-built houses in the area are of limestone.

Historians' claims that Kepier was the source of at least some of the cathedral's building stone are refuted by some geologists. Admittedly there is evidence of much stone extraction around the peninsula, although quality is a factor not to be overlooked.

The Ordnance Survey Map of 1895 shows that the Kepier quarry nearest the city was then the sole survivor and was approached by roads from both Kepier and Gilesgate Moor via High Grange Farm, although this route involved crossing the railway line which ran into Gilesgate Station.

There is on record an account of an accident at this crossing in June 1844. Mr Jackson, a city mason, with his cart and horses, was crossing the Durham Branch Line, heading for Kepier quarries when the 9 o'clock train from Newcastle came up suddenly and hit them. Both horses were killed instantly but the driver miraculously escaped with only a few bruises.

Today, a walk through Kepier woods doesn't involve such risks. The railway closed in 1966 and the quarries stand in a silence broken only by the sound of waterfalls tumbling through the old

workings. They have been modified by nature into a wonderful riverside haven for a wide variety of wild flowers, animals and woodland birds.

Kepier quarries.

Belmont Viaduct

WHEN the North-Eastern Railway decided to build a line to service the coalfield at Crook, which, at that time, was the sole preserve of its rival, the Stockton & Darlington Railway, they chose a route from the 'Old Main Line' near Leamside, which would take them down the Wear valley via Durham and Bishop Auckland. This route required the building of five high viaducts, and although part of the line has been closed since 1964, four of them still stand. Two of them were incorporated into the new main line, now the East Coast Main Line between London and Edinburgh, one at Durham and the other over the River Browney and Relley Mill to the south of Durham.

The Newton Cap Viaduct near Bishop Auckland, which carried the main line over the River Wear, has been cleverly converted to a road bridge, and where steam trains, and later diesel units, hurtled their way 120ft above the river, now cars, lorries and buses find it an easier route instead of descending to the bottom and climbing out again.

Belmont viaduct, crossing the River Wear.

The remaining viaduct, which also crosses the Wear, is near Durham, the Belmont Viaduct. It remains untouched, standing as built in 1856. It looks very forlorn above the riverside footpath, because it has no use. It is barred at both ends, there is no footpath across it, nor is there ever likely to be, because what remains of the route runs out within a quarter of a mile, into the A1(M) motorway. It doesn't leap across the river, but gently strides over with its eight arches, giving it a certain elegance in the wooded gorge. Because it can only be viewed from below, its height of 130ft makes it look very impressive, as was the desire of the mid-19th-century railway architects, in this case a Mr Cail of Newcastle.

Man was conquering distance and reducing time, striding over mere obstacles such as a river and its gorge.

Brasside Ponds

ONCE the scene of great brickmaking activity, this area became yet another site of industrial waste and desolation.

The transformation is now complete. Nature has done her work well, producing from these extensive claypits as tranquil a sanctuary as bird or man could wish.

There was brick, tile and pipe manufacturing at Brasside in 1864, although earlier working may pre-date this recording. Certainly brickmaking began in the area much earlier because bricks were used in Durham Castle in about 1500.

The walker on the Weardale Way will wish to linger awhile here, unaware that he or she is an intruder in the hidden eyes of the resident wildlife which have wisely chosen this secluded, attractive

The picturesque Brasside ponds.

hideaway on the out-skirts of Durham City.

Finchale Priory

FINCHALE Priory is set in a secluded spot on a bend in the River Wear, about four miles from Durham City. The steep river banks, covered in rich, hanging foliage, seem to strive to hide the ruin from view.

Some historians believe that this is the place where Ethelwald, King of Northumbria, died in 765 AD. It is also thought that a synod was held here in 792 by Higbald, Bishop of Lindisfarne, for the reg-

Finchale Priory, built on the site of St Godric's hermitage.

Finchale Priory.

ulation of church discipline. This was supposedly followed by two further meetings for the same purpose in 798 and 810.

Finchale is, perhaps, better known for its association with St Godric. In the 12th century it became the home of this remarkable man. He was born in Walpole in Norfolk in 1065 and for the early part of his adult life was a successful pedlar. Later he became part-owner of a coasting vessel and made his living as a sea trader. On one of these voyages he visited Lindisfarne — the story of St Cuthbert had a profound effect on him and directly he made a pilgrimage to Jerusalem. He also made a further pilgrimage to Rome accompanied by his mother. He eventually settled near the market town of Wolsingham, in Weardale, as a disciple of Alric, a hermit who is reputed to have shared his cave with a pack of savage wolves. Godric stayed for two years and when Alric died he made another pilgrimage to the Holy Land.

On his return he settled for a while near Whitby and eventually came to Durham where he became sacrist at St Giles' Church. It was here, we are told, that he learned to read and write. His desire to be a hermit was still strong and he chose to settle in a 'snake-infested' place, near Finchale, granted to him by Bishop Flambard. He built himself a hut and a small oratory which he dedicated to St Mary. It was, perhaps, a strange hermitage because his mother, brother and sister followed him to Finchale. His mother died shortly afterwards and his brother was drowned in the River Wear, but his sister lived nearby for many years in a cell near to his hermitage.

On moving to Finchale, Godric observed all the austerities of a hermit.

He used a stone for his pillow and his table. He would only eat food when it was rotten and his bread was made half of flour and half of ashes. He excavated a bath in the bare ground at the river edge and would often stand naked, up to his neck in cold water, praying all night. The deadly poisonous snakes did not bother him and, indeed, they would come into his hut and would even entwine themselves around his legs to keep warm in the cold weather. He was robbed and almost killed by a band of invading Scots in 1138, and in 1149 his home was almost washed away in a great flood. In gratitude for it being saved, he built a bigger oratory which was dedicated to St John the Baptist by Bishop William de St Barbara.

Every Sunday and holy day a monk from Durham would come to celebrate mass in his oratory. For the last few years of his life Godric was confined to his bed and lived only on milk. He died on 21 May 1170, at the age of 105, and was buried in his oratory.

County Durham's most notable monastic ruin, Finchale Priory.

After his death, Finchale was at first occupied by one monk and later two monks took up residence, these were Henry and Reginald, who was his biographer.

In 1241 the Archbishop of York ordered the building of a church at Finchale and this became a 'holiday home' for the monks of Durham who came on a rota system, four at a time, to join the five resident monks.

Unfortunately their behaviour seems to have been less than holy because they were severely reprimanded for keeping a pack of hounds and, a century later, for wearing linen shirts instead of their habits.

In the general upheaval that came with the Dissolution, St Godric's body vanished. However, the site of his empty tomb is marked by a stone cross set into the floor of the nave.

Finchale Priory is now in the care of English Heritage and is, perhaps, County Durham's most notable monastic ruin.

St Lawrence, Pittington.

Church of St Lawrence, Pittington

THE parish church of St Lawrence at Pittington Hallgarth deserves a visit for so many reasons.

Its setting, in a wooded burial ground, is truly a picture in all seasons. Once inside the gates, a feeling of awe descends upon the hesitant visitor but the ancient stonework is beckoning through the trees and just past the impressive war memorial, the porch, which tends to hide the Norman door, extends a welcome.

The key obtained nearby, the church opens to an unexpected treasure of architectural and artistic features unparalleled in the county and in some aspects seeming to vie with Durham Cathedral, although on a more humble scale.

One remarkable feature is the pair of adjacent wall-paintings believed to be of 11th or 12th century origin showing the consecration of St Cuthbert and his

Wall-painting of the consecration of St Cuthbert, Church of St Lawrence, Pittington.

vision at the table of the Abbess Elfled.

Here is an example of time standing still and the visitor may well feel inclined to just stand and try to drink it all in, to become part of it. However much time has been allowed, it will seem inadequate for this exquisite architectural gem. A simple church guide, normally available, will be invaluable and almost surely guarantee a return visit.

Brancepeth Castle

THE history of Brancepeth Castle dates back to pre-Conquest times when the Saxon family of Bulmer owned the land. Soon after the Norman invasion it passed to the Nevilles, by the marriage of a Bulmer heiress. It was Ralph Neville, the 1st Earl of Westmorland, who built the castle at the end of the 14th century. The Neville occupation of the castle ended with the 5th Earl's involve-

ment in 'The Rising of the North', the ill-fated attempt to restore the Roman Catholic religion and put Mary, Queen of Scots, on the English throne. The estate stayed with the Crown until James I granted it to Robert Carr, or Kerr, a member of the notorious Border Reiver family, but nevertheless a royal favourite. James made him Earl of Somerset and also, when the estate was granted to him, Baron Brancepeth. His career, however, came to an abrupt end when it was found that he, and his equally notorious wife, had instigated the murder of Sir Thomas Overbury.

The estate was eventually purchased by Ralph Cole, a wealthy businessman from Gateshead. However, it was sold by his grandson, Sir Ralph, because of severe financial difficulties. The castle then came into the ownership of Sir Henry Bellasis, whose daughter is remembered as the sweetheart of 'Bonnie Bobbie Shafto' in the famous song.

William Russell, a wealthy Sunderland banker, was the next owner and he spent more than £120,000 rebuilding the castle. The architect employed was John Patterson of Edinburgh, whose efforts, to say the least, caused great dismay among experts. And even

The Gateway, Brancepeth Castle.

though the celebrated restorer of Alnwick Castle, John Salvin, was brought in to try to rectify the mistakes, the final result is still regarded as less than satisfactory.

The castle eventually came into the possession, by marriage, of the family of Viscount Boyne. It has, in more recent times, served as the headquarters for the Durham Light Infantry, and as a research establishment for Jobling Glassware from Sunderland, manufacturers of the famous 'Pyrex'.

St Brandon's Church, Brancepeth

ST BRANDON'S Church, Brancepeth, is reputed to be one of only two in the country dedicated to this Celtic saint. Brandon, or Brendan, the navigator, sailed the high seas in a leather boat in the 5th century, and some historians believe he even sailed to North America.

It was at this attractive country church that John Cosin was rector before he was chosen as Prince Bishop of Durham in 1660, at the age of 64. He was the first Prince Bishop after the Restoration and strove to repair all the ravages committed during the Com-

St Brandon's Church entrance (left) and nave (right).

monwealth. Throughout his diocese he urged the restoration of ruined churches and chapels; he revived the church services and even rewrote the Common Prayer Book. He became rector of St Brandon's in 1625 and it was he who was directly responsible for the elaborate woodwork of the altar, choir, pews, pulpit and font cover in the church.

As could be expected, because of its proximity to the castle, some notable members of the Neville family are commemorated by monuments in the church. In the north transept there are two finely carved oak effigies of Ralph Neville, the 2nd Earl of Westmorland, and his second wife, Margaret, daughter of Reginald, Lord Cobham. The earl was a quiet and gentle member of this family which was constantly involved in bitter conflict. He died peacefully in 1484 during the reign of Henry VII.

Another remarkable effigy can be seen in the chancel. This impressive stone figure, almost 8ft in length, is of Robert Neville who was known as 'the Peacock of the North' because of his love for fine clothes. He was killed at Berwick in 1319, while fighting against the Scots for Edward II, and was brought back to Brancepeth for burial. He was a naturally argumentative character and once slew one of his kinsmen during an altercation on Framwellgate Bridge in Durham City.

This beautiful little church is mainly 12th to 14th century in construction, and additions from subsequent cen-

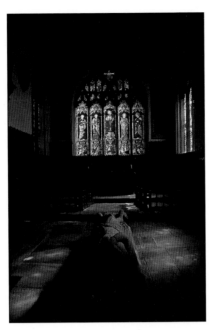

turies are in evidence. However, its chief wonder must be John Cosin's glorious Restoration woodwork which richly adorns the interior.

The chancel with the tomb of Sir Robert Neville, St Brandon's Church, Brancepeth.

Croxdale Hall Norman Church

THE half-mile walk from Sunderland Bridge through the parkland to Croxdale Hall is a very pleasant and rewarding exercise. The Norman church behind the Hall is a surprising bonus.

Due to deterioration inside, it is unfortunately only possible to view it externally, over the churchyard wall. There is, however, much to note, not least the Norman doorway with the

Croxdale's Norman Church.

Croxdale Church's Norman doorway, with Tree of Life carving in the tympanum.

apparently original door complete with ornate iron hinge strapwork. In the tympanum, the carving is now quite heavily weathered but is still discernible as a representation of the tree of life.

Originally built as one of four chapels of ease to St Oswald's parish, Durham, it was inherited by the Catholic family of Salvins when they came to Croxdale in 1402. They built the-present Croxdale Hall in about 1760. In 1807 they added a substantial chapel in Gothic style, integral with the Hall and almost opposite the small Norman church.

In 1845, when the Dean and Chapter sought land upon which to build a larger and more conveniently located church, the Salvins provided the present site of St Bartholomew at Sunderland Bridge and in exchange received the old church, which then unfortunately fell into disuse. However, the churchyard was used for family burials and the church fabric has recently been thoroughly restored.

Eastern County Durham

Signing Bank, near Cassop

THE high vantage point of Signing Bank affords a magnificent view across the eastern Durham countryside towards Durham City.

The bank is part of an ancient routeway. It was here, when travelling on this road, that pilgrims on their way to visit the Shrine of St Cuthbert would have their first sighting of Durham Cathedral and would kneel and make the sign of the cross — hence the name — Signing Bank.

In contrast, the adjacent Witch Hill is where, in the 17th century, at the height of superstitious persecutions, witches were tried and burned.

Ludworth Tower

DESPITE Durham's distance from the Scottish border it did not escape the Scots' ambitions. Ludworth Tower is a memorial of those times when sufficiently wealthy landowners built themselves a refuge for their family and livestock.

This pele tower was extended by the

The City of Durham, from Signing Bank.

Remains of Lud-worth Tower.

Holdens who had held the estate since 1411. It became their manor house and a licence to embattle and turret it was granted by Bishop Langley in 1422.

Its dramatic though scant remains reward close examination, for despite its major collapse late last century, much survives to aid our mental reconstruction. The tunnel-vaulted ground floor for cattle; the lower treads of the spiral stone staircase, so defendable; fireplaces on at least two floors and embrasured window openings scanning the descending countryside begin to give us an indication of conditions in a beleaguered pele tower in the 14th century.

Bishop Thomas Langley was elected a cardinal by Pope John XIII. He died in France in 1437.

Haswell Engine House

TODAY the stark ruined pumping engine house at Haswell Plough is all that remains here to indicate Haswell's past importance in County Durham's coal mining history.

Sunk in 1831, its high quality steam coal ensured development and prosperity for the village. However, its reputation as the birthplace of the 'Haswell Mechanical Coalgetter' together with developing technology to overcome flooding, could not solve this major problem and the colliery was forced to close in 1895.

This ruin has, however, a far greater significance as an on-site memorial to 95 men and boys who died 150 fathoms below on 28 September 1844 when an

Remains of the Haswell engine house.

explosion of gas in this highly regarded mine sent a deadly flame throughout that section known as 'The Little Pit'. It destroyed the ventilation system by demolishing the air stoppings designed to channel the fresh air as required. Fifteen died from burns, the remainder from the resultant afterdamp.

Most were laid to rest in South Hetton Churchyard, the ceremonies extending over two days. There would barely be a household in the immediate area not depleted by this tragedy and many of them would be suddenly bereft of any income. One widow was left mourning her husband and three sons.

After 150 years have elapsed, during which the colliery site has been cleared beyond recognition, it is quite remarkable to find that their memory lives on in a most worthy form. The church hall, attached to South Hetton Parish Church is dedicated to them and there-

in the tragedy is suitably documented that they may never be forgotten.

St Helen's Church, Kelloe

ST HELEN'S Church in Kelloe is a fine example of a Norman church. It was founded in the 13th century as the chantry of the Kellow family, from whom the nearby village takes its name. Richard Kellow became Prince Bishop of Durham in 1311 and ruled for five turbulent years, up to his death at Bishop Middleham in 1316.

The interior of the church contains many items of historical interest. The bells are over 700 years old and are still used regularly. A beautifully restored coat-of-arms, dating from about 1680, which belonged to Charles II is also on display.

Perhaps the most wonderful treasure of the church is the Kelloe Cross.

St Helen's Church, Kelloe.

Regarded as one of the finest Norman sculptures in County Durham, it depicts St Helen finding the true cross.

The church also has a strong connection with Elizabeth Barrett Browning. Her family lived in the nearby but now demolished Coxhoe Hall and she was baptised in the font that is still in use today. Her gentle style of poetry seems to find empathy with the tranquil setting of the church on the gently sloping valley side of the Kelloe Beck:

'How do I love thee? Let me count the ways.
I love thee to the depth and breadth and height
My soul can reach, when feeling out of sight
For the ends of Being and ideal Grace.
Love thee to the level of every day's
Most quiet need, by sun and candle-light.
I love thee freely, as men strive for Right;
I love thee purely, as they turn from Praise.
I love thee with a passion put to use
In my old griefs, and with my childhood's faith.
I love thee with a love I seemed to lose
With my lost saints, — I love thee with the breath,
Smiles, tears, all my life! — and, if God choose,
I shall but love thee better after death.'

Sonnet XLIII, from *The Portuguese*
Elizabeth Barrett Browning

Church of St Mary Magdalene, Trimdon Village

ST MARY'S Church, Trimdon, was founded in 1145 AD by a group of Augustinian monks from Guisborough Priory who farmed a little to the south of what is now the village green. This place was called 'Tremadune' — 'The Cross On The Hill' — and it is from this that the present village takes its name. Unfortunately no early records of this settlement exist because they were burned by a monk seeking revenge for his dismissal from Guisborough.

Local legend tells of a secret tunnel leading from the church to the site of the farm. It was thought that this had been discovered early in 1989 when the chancel floor was being prepared for the fitting of a new carpet. However, the discovery turned out to be a family burial vault containing five coffins — four of adults and one of a child. Although this is believed to be the Beckwith family vault, there is evidence in the parish records to suggest that members of the Donnison family may also be interred. However, any connection between the two families is uncertain. It is known that the Beckwiths were powerful landowners in the area during the 18th century and a descendant of the family is still a regular attender of the church.

Horseshoe-shaped chancel arch, St Mary Magdalene.

This attractively situated church has many interesting features, including a medieval bellcote and a 'leper window' —a window placed and angled so that lepers, who were not allowed inside the church, could see the altar to worship without being seen by the congregation. St Mary's is also unique in that it boasts what is reputedly the only horseshoe-shaped chancel arch in Christendom.

Trimdon Village itself is famous as the place from which, in 1017, King Cnut set out on his famous barefoot pilgrimage to the Shrine of St Cuthbert in Durham.

Shotton Hall, Peterlee

SHOTTON Hall is a fine example of an 18th-century country house. It stands in shady, wooded grounds in the village of Old Shotton on the edge of the New Town of Peterlee.

Church of St Mary Magdalene, Trimdon Village.

Shotton Hall, Peterlee.

The land on which the house is built belonged to a family of gentlemen farmers named Thompson. The family heiress, Elizabeth, married Charles Brandling, a Gosforth business man, and in 1756 the Hall was built as a home for the newly-weds. They eventually became the largest landowners in the area and the size of the house was increased, as befitted their position.

The last in line of the Brandlings was born in 1798, and he, too, was named Charles but was unfortunately ruined by mining speculation in the Haswell area and was forced to sell off his estates, including the Hall, to the Shotton Coal Company, to pay off his debts. The Coal Company were not interested in the Hall direct-ly, but worked the rich coal seam beneath.

The Hall passed into the hands of the Burdon family in 1880 and remained in their possession until the outbreak of World War Two in 1939, when it was requisitioned by the War Office.

After the war it became the head-quarters of the Peterlee Development Corporation, and, after their demise was bought by Peterlee Town Council.

Shotton Hall is reputed to be haunt-ed by a 'Grey Lady' — the ghost of a servant girl who suffered an indiscre-tion with one of the masters of the house. Grief stricken, she hanged her-self and it is said she can still be seen climbing the stairs to the servants' quarters, the scene of the tragedy.

Castle Eden Dene

PERHAPS the most attractive natural features of the Durham coastline are its several denes whose burns have been cutting their way through the magnesian limestone since the last Ice Age. Of these, Castle Eden Dene is undoubtedly the longest, at four miles, and the largest, covering 500 acres.

It would seem that man has been enjoying the dene for many thousands of years, since traces of his occupation, in the form of flints shaped into tools, have been found all along this stretch of coastline. In 1150, after centuries of changing ownerships, Robert De Brus, Lord of The Manor of Eden, built a 'castle' in the dene and the village of Eden, whose name is derived from Yoden, the medieval village where Peterlee now stands, became known as Castle Eden.

In 1757 Rowland Burdon of the successful Stockton family bought the estate, although the castle, possibly only a fortified manor house, was by then quite ruinous. He began building a new residence which was to serve his descendants for nearly 200 years. The dene itself was an integral part of his plans and Burdon's son built a road through the dene from the castle to the sea, as only the beginning of a complex development over the years ahead.

On the very brink of the dene is one of Durham's hidden treasures, St James' Church. The original structure was built in accordance with Robert De Brus' charter of 1150 as a chapel for the village of Eden, but having deteriorated was rebuilt by Rowland Burdon in 1764 with the addition of a steeple. His son extended it with two aisles and, indeed, most of the embellishment and

The 'castle' at Castle Eden.

*St James' Church,
Castle Eden.*

furnishings of the church is attributable to successive generations of the Burdon family.

In 1850 Burdon's descendants opened up their beloved dene to the public and today it offers opportunities to see rare examples of wildlife, flora and fauna such as cannot be expected to be found grouped in one compact area anywhere else in County Durham. Peterlee Development Corporation took over ownership in 1951, very conscious of the dene's prestige and determined to preserve its natural state. In 1954 the dene was designated a local nature reserve and remains a truly enviable asset incorporated into the new town.

Seaton Holme, Easington Village

THIS former rectory is believed to be one of the oldest surviving domestic buildings in England. The earliest portions of the east wing have been defined as mid-13th century and evidence of an earlier timber manor on the site appears to indicate Saxon origins. Much rebuilding, extension and demolition over the centuries has resulted in a site of considerable complexity and intrigue.

By this century the rectory had become quite unsuitable. The parish had diminished and there were no longer tithes coming in to support such opulence. A new rectory was built in the extensive grounds to the west and the old rectory was sold in 1921 to the Board of Guardians and became known as Seaton Holme. It was first used as a children's home to relieve the workhouse in the village but later became a hostel for men. The Social Services then devoted it to various uses but it was eventually abandoned when it deteriorated, seemingly beyond redemption.

Now bought and restored by Easington Parish Council, it has been awarded Grade 1 listed status and serves the village as a most remarkable community centre. It provides offices for the Parish Council, and the East Durham Groundwork Trust, which works in close collaboration with them, also occupies part of the building.

The outstanding facility incorporated into this community building is the Discovery Centre where residents, and visitors to East Durham, can investigate the history of the area and can discover the early importance of Easington. Since earliest times, centuries before all the neighbouring present-day parishes

The former rectory, now Seaton Holme, Easington Village.

were detached to become parishes in their own right, Easington was the capital of the Ward and Deanery which covered from the Wear to Hart.

From 1256 until 1832, the rectors of Easington enjoyed the dual appointment of Archdeacon of Durham and, in view of the importance and prestige of this position, they were selected from families of substance. This explains the size and grandeur of the Easington Rectory, adapted and improved by successive rectors over the centuries. They were also in a prime position for promotion, working directly under the bishop, and indeed acting frequently upon his behalf so that many of them progressed to positions of high authority within the Church.

No doubt, years ago, the villagers would approach the rectory in trepidation, pull the bell at the gate in the high, forbidding stone wall which enclosed the grounds, and wonder who might appear.

Today, the perimeter wall has gone, and the now gleaming white 'Old Rectory' beams a great welcome across the grass to the villagers and visitors who can all find a very good reason for just popping in, unannounced. Congratulations to Easington Parish Council for the transformation.

The cemetery and the nearby memorial avenue at Easington Colliery.

Easington Colliery Disaster Memorial

A PLEASANT tree-lined stroll just off the main street of Easington Colliery, suddenly takes on a sombre aspect when we pause halfway along this traffic-free haven. A bronze plaque has caught our attention and tells us that each of these 83 mature trees was planted in memory of a miner, man or boy, lost in the Easington Colliery Disaster on 29 May 1951.

Tommy Mothersill still lives in the village and recalls that morning. He went down the shaft with his mates at 5.00am, and gradually realised something was wrong. A putrid smell was engulfing the cage. At the bottom they were ordered to return to the surface. The village slept on, unaware there had been a serious explosion about 4.30am.

"How we'd been allowed to descend so far I'll never know," says Tommy. *"We started the rescue operation but all we brought out was bodies. Some were my friends. I was just 21. All but a very few were buried in a communal grave in Easington Colliery Cemetery"*

The memorial is lovingly attended by families to this day. The inscription makes poignant reading. It is a message to all who have ever burned coal.

Beacon Hill, Easington

JUST north of the village of Easington is Beacon Hill, the highest point on the dramatic Durham coast. Rising to over 250ft above the North Sea and covering about 34 acres, this superb vantage point offers spectacular views north and south. The hill has been in the care of the National Trust since 1987 when it was purchased with Enterprise Neptune funds and grants from the Countryside Commission and Nature Conservancy Council.

In the days of the great sailing ships, fires were lit here to warn sailors of the dangerous reefs that project at this point.

One story tells of a ship with 50 crew being lost on 25 November 1825 on a treacherous reef known as the 'Skaw' which projects from the nearby bay of Hawthorn Hive.

Blackhall Rocks

A LITTLE south of the coastal village of Blackhall, a road leads down to the sea. The Blackhall Rocks are the natural development of coastal erosion over the centuries.

Cavernous openings in the cliffs and isolated portions of earlier mainland, now themselves tunnelled through by the action of the relentless tides, form attractive shorescapes for visitors, local people and artists.

In 1916 there was an interesting find at Blackhall. This was the discovery of a

Durham's highest coastal point, Beacon Hill, Easington.

Blackhall Rocks, on Durham's spectacular coastline

The remains of Dalden Tower, Seaham.

pagan child's burial, contained within a stone cist. The only other find within the grave was one bead, which may have been left by accident. It is possible that the burial was Anglo-Saxon, although the position of the body and the lack of additional goods in the grave suggest that it may possibly date from the Iron Age or even Bronze Age.

Dalden Tower

A PELE tower ruin of considerable size, indicating the extent of the original site, is to be found in Dalton-le-Dale. It now serves as a sheltered picnic area in this typical Durham dene which reaches the coast at Seaham Harbour.

The Norman family of Escolland obtained licence to crenellate their manor house, Dalden Hall, towards the end of the reign of Edward II (1307-27). Contemporary records indicate

property of some substance, referring to a bailey providing for a chapel, among other buildings. Sir Jordan de Dalton, who took his family name from the estate, successfully applied to have a chantry for his chapel, but in order to protect the parish church there were strict conditions:

Masses were only to be said for family, their guests and servants.

Parishoners would not be allowed to use the chapel.

Sir Jordan and his family were to attend mass at the parish church (St Andrew's) on a specified number of occasions each year.

Sir Jordan was required to provide the church with wax for candle-making.

Through the generations Dalden passed, by marriage, into the Bowes family of Streatlam, then to the Collingwoods and eventually to the Londonderrys, but by this time the property had been abandoned and was fast advancing towards its present state.

Incredible though it may seem, there is a tradition that the tower is connected to the coast by a secret tunnel. More probably the reality is that a short tunnel emerged nearby, at a safe distance, to enable escape to the coast in those threatening times.

'Sundial' in the Church of St Andrew, Dalton-le-Dale.

Dalton-le-Dale

TO the hasty traveller, passing through the dale, the small but attractive church of St Andrew is almost lost in the trees. But why hasten through such a delightful, sheltered stretch of village with its houses scattered along the brook which passes Dalden Tower to soon meet the North Sea? Time should be allocated for a leisurely exploration.

The recently restored, stream-fed horse trough, arched over by the ancient churchyard wall, recalls those days of more leisurely transport when up to 20 ponies and traps would assemble at this point, offering themselves for hire up and down the dale and to surrounding towns and villages, Trapping, it was called.

The church is of Norman origin but has received constant attention through the centuries as evidenced by its many datable features. These include a recumbent stone effigy in full armour, set into an arched recess in the nave's north wall. It is interpreted as Sir William Bowes, who married Maude, the heiress of the Dalden family in 1375, whereupon Dalden became the Bowes family's favourite retreat.

However, the church's most curious attraction is surely the internal 'sundial'. This simply comprised a range of boldly projecting Roman numerals, spaced out along the north wall of the nave, at wainscot level. With the help of a beam of sunshine progressing slowly along, west to east, the time was indicated.

Apparently this ancient clock ceased to function when the church roof was altered and a plaster ceiling inserted, thereby eliminating the aperture designed to provide the sunbeam. The considerable distance between the numerals could have offered great accuracy as the intervals may have been further divided into minutes, simply painted in, but long since obliterated.

Be that as it may, as the sunbeam crept towards the pulpit, there would be no excuse for the preacher to exceed his normal length of sermon.

Seaham

FOR generations of fishermen returning to the tiny village of Seaham, the cliff-top silhouette of St Mary's Church would have been a reassuring sight, forecasting the calm and security they had anticipated since launching their cobles.

Originally Saxon, St Mary's Church was built in many stages. Nave only,

Seaham Hall, Seaham.

then chancel added and the whole embattled as one. Tower, porch, the roof lowered, buttresses to the rescue and windows re-ordered. Building material was a combination of sand-stones and limestones involving every variety of finish from rubble, herring-bone, to squared ashlar coursing. A substantial amount of the nave's walling is obviously re-used Roman material, probably recovered from one of the Roman signalling stations that once ranged down this coastline. It is said that walls have ears but these walls can talk and tell us a great deal. Can we interpret it all and in the correct sequence? Perhaps it is safest to listen to the sundial dated 1773 over the south entrance porch. The severely weathered inscription describes itself:

'The natural clockwork by the mighty one
Wound up at first and ever since has gone.
No pin drops out, its wheels and springs hold good.
It speaks its maker's praise, tho' once it stood;
But that was by the order of the work-man's power,
And when it stands again it goes no more.'

In 1820, Sir Ralph Milbanke, who had recently adopted the surname 'Noel', approached the eminent civil engineer William Chapman to prepare plans for the construction of a har-bour near Seaham on the coast of his County Durham estate. He had the foresight to realise that the series of

St Mary's Church, Seaham.

coves on this desolate and dangerous coastline, lent themselves to such a development, although previously renowned only for shipwrecks and smuggling. Inland, coalmining was fast expanding, but the new industry's major problem was transporting the output to the coast for shipment to London. Before anything materialised from these plans, Lord Charles Henry Stewart, upon seeing them, realised how advantageous the scheme could be for his wife's collieries. He had just married Lady Frances Anne Vane Tempest who had inherited her father's vast estate, Wynyard Park, together with coal mines at Rainton and Pittington. Upon hearing that Sir Ralph was selling his Seaham estate, the Stewarts bought it at auction late in

1821 and immediately instructed Chapman to prepare a much more ambitious plan. They were spurred on by the incentive of avoiding the cost of moving their coal, first by rail to the staithes at Penshaw, then by keel to Sunderland where it was again transferred to a seagoing vessel and involved port handling charges.

In future they would be able to lay a railway direct from their collieries to Seaham, only four miles away, and ship out of a purpose-built harbour, unaffected by river-mouth flooding.

At that time Lady Stewart was the second largest exporter of coal through the port of Sunderland, totalling a quarter of a million tons a year from her own collieries. But the new port facility would be open to other coal-

The north harbour, Seaham.

owners. A venture such as this, however, was to require considerable financial investment and so it was not until the summer of 1828 that actual construction commenced. During the intervening years, Wynyard Park had almost completely burned down and together with the extensive rebuilding of their London home, Holderness House, their resources were severely drained.

On 28 November 1828, Lord Stewart, or the Marquess of Londonderry as he had become upon the death of Lord Castlereagh, laid the foundation stone of the North Pier and on the same day his seven-year-old eldest son, Viscount

Following this, the inner harbour was blasted out and railways connected from the collieries so that by July 1831 two sets of loading gear were able to demonstrate to the Marquess and his supporters, the procedure of loading coals into the new vessel, *Lord Seaham*, which promptly put to sea for the London market.

The Marquess had achieved his ambition. History having been made, he and his party could retire to Seaham Hall to celebrate in the grand manner.

Durham coal was being shipped out of Seaham Harbour and progressively, over the years, the harbour would be extended and improved beyond the Marquess' most optimistic expectations. Eventually the port of Sunderland would be connected by the Londonderry Railway in 1854, the year of his death.

Seaham Hall would have been originally built as a manor house and was still referred to as Seaham House, even after it was rebuilt by the Milbanke family in 1792, at which time it would consist only of the central section of today's front elevation. It was, however, the core of the small range of properties fronting on to the village green of Seaham, later to become known as 'Old Seaham'.

The ancient family of Milbanke had bought the estate from the Collingwoods — descendants of the Bowes family — who had also owned the adjacent Dalden. But Yorkshire baronet Sir Ralph Milbanke, who had been MP for County Durham, was financially strained by this time. He had incurred considerable electioneering expenditure and he was funding a dowry for his daughter. Anne Isabella was married to

Seaham, laid the foundation stone of the first house in Seaham New Town. The North Pier would eventually form the outer harbour. The work progressed quickly. The limestone rock which was dug out was immediately processed into lime or used as a filling, in the construction of the pier.

Lord Byron, the poet, in the upstairs drawing room at the Hall in 1815. As predicted, the marriage was not a success and broke up within the year. Under these circumstances, and despite plans to develop Seaham as a coal port to serve all the nearby collieries, Sir Ralph put his Hall and his estate up for auction. On 13 October 1821 it was bought by Lord Stewart and his young wife.

During the early years of their marriage they lived in Vienna where Lord Stewart was Britain's ambassador, and later at Wynyard Park where Lady Stewart found on her return that the contents had been gradually removed over the years by her mother, the Countess of Antrim.

Having been brought up in the magnificence of Wynyard Park, and now free to occupy it once more, together with a fine London mansion, it is not surprising that Lady Stewart considered Seaham Hall to be inconveniently small.

She reputedly referred to it as 'The Cottage' when not being even more disparaging. However, residing there allowed the Marquess and Marchioness of Londonderry ready access to their developing business interests and, equally important, as they saw it, their responsibilities — the collieries, railways and harbour. Living there also enabled them to supervise progress on the building work which resulted from their worthwhile benevolence towards their workers, the people of Seaham. Churches, infirmary, schools and all manner of buildings for recreational purposes were being built and continuously maintained at their expense.

After Lord Londonderry died at their London home in 1854, Lady Londonderry continued to exercise her remarkable business acumen to advance her various interests, showing herself to be far ahead of her time. She spent a greater part of each year at Seaham Hall and in 1859 she planned the removal of the road running inland from the coast so that the Hall would enjoy greater privacy and the grounds could extend, uninterrupted, down to the dene. Consequently a new road was constructed north of the Hall and this, together with improved landscaping, was completed in the early 1860s. Lady Londonderry began to enlarge the Hall by extending to east and west, tolerating no existing structures to impede the progress of her plans.

Even the Home Farm was demolished and resited to allow development. As before, she used the Hall and grounds to offer the grandest hospitality, not only to great personalities, but also to her 4,000 workers, displaying her appreciation and admiration.

Her exhausting lifestyle eventually took its toll and she died at Seaham Hall a few days after her 65th birthday. The family retained Seaham Hall until 1927 when the 7th Marquess, perpetuating his ancestors' concern for the health of the people of Seaham, presented the now vast building to Durham County Council for use as a tuberculosis sanatorium.

Happily there is no longer such a need and Seaham Hall is now returned to private ownership, but the town, while ennobled by its history has sadly, lost its noble founders.

Northern County Durham

Chester-le-Street

AS its name suggests, the market town of Chester-le-Street dates from Roman times. They had a fort here, occupying some six or seven acres. It housed a cavalry regiment which guarded the road that their engineers had constructed from Binchester to Newcastle. Roman relics have been found from time to time and some can be seen on display in the Parish Church of St Mary and St Cuthbert which is situated at the centre of the site of the Roman fort.

Chester-le-Street has a prominent place in the history of County Durham as one of the long-term resting places of St Cuthbert's remains. In 875 AD the monks of Lindisfarne, under the threat of Norse invaders, fled from their island sanctuary taking with them the coffin of St Cuthbert. For eight years they wandered all over the north with their precious burden, until at last they came to Chester-le-Street in 883 AD. They built a wooden cathedral in which to place the body of their saint and other treasures. St Cuthbert's body rested here for 113 years and the town was the centre of a vast diocese extending from the North Sea to the Irish Sea and from the River Tees to the Firth of Forth. During this period the town was the seat of nine Saxon bishops and the shrine of St Cuthbert was richly endowed with fine gifts from many notable visitors and benefactors.

Among these was King Athelstan who, in 937 AD, sought the aid of St Cuthbert for his forthcoming battle with the Scots. He brought many gifts, such as chalices, plates, tapestries, curtains, gospels, four bells, and a cross of gold. His half-brother, who succeeded him as King Edmund, gave robes and two of his own gold arm bracelets, when he visited the shrine.

In 995 AD the monks were again under the threat of Norse invasion and they set forth once more bearing the

Lumley's warriors (left) and the magnificent stained-glass windows (right) St Mary and St Cuthbert's Church, Chester-le-Street.

St Mary and St Cuthbert's Church, Chester-le-Street.

church should be built. While the foundations were being dug, the treasury of the Roman garrison was uncovered, containing a hoard of gold. Egelric claimed this for himself and swiftly departed to his native Peterborough. Despite putting his new-found wealth to charitable use the question of his integrity was raised again, after the Conquest, by William the Conqueror. He was imprisoned in the Tower of London, and while awating trail he died.

Egelric's church was almost completely rebuilt in the late 13th century when the Bishop of Durham, Anthony Bek, raised it to the status of a collegiate church with a dean, seven canons, five chaplains, three deacons, and other ministers.

At the Reformation it became an ordinary parish church again, but was restored to a Rectory in 1865. Against the north wall of the tower is a small stone building of two floors, dating from the 13th century. This was the cell or anchorage of a hermit or anker. It is thought to be one of the best preserved anchorages in England. An anchorite would be walled up for life to pass his time in prayer and contemplation. A narrow slit in the wall of the upper floor would allow him to see the altar in

coffin of St Cuthbert. This time they found sanctuary at Ripon, staying with the religious community there for a month until the danger had passed. On their return, as the legend has it, a new resting place for the saint was revealed to them in a vision, at Dunholme, or Durham, where the mighty Norman cathedral now stands. Following this transfer to Durham, Chester-le-Street declined in importance and its church gradually became a ruin.

It remained in this condition until just before the Norman Conquest when Bishop Egelric decided that a new the south aisle, whilst another opening allowed food to be passed to him from the tower.

After the Reformation this 'Anker's House' became an almshouse for poor widows, but in 1626 the curate, Roger Willis, wanted to use it as his home. He tried to evict the widows and even obtained a warrant from Durham to give them a ducking on the ducking-stool. However, the ladies held their own and were eventually allowed to stay.

The church remains, for the people of Chester-le-Street, a source of great pride, being both a house of prayer and a reminder that their history reaches back nearly 2,000 years to the Roman occupation.

On a stone bench, along the wall of the north aisle of the church, is a line of 14 stone effigies supposedly of members of the Lumley family. These are known locally as 'Lumley's Warriors' and were placed here in 1594 by John, Lord Lumley, to honour and commemorate his ancestors. He lived in the nearby Lumley Castle, just a mile to the east. It is an impressive sight standing four-square with its yellow stone battlements soaring above the trees. The history of the Lumleys dates back to the time of Edward the Confessor but the greater part of the castle dates from the end of the 14th century. It was Ralph Lumley, created the first Baron Lumley by Richard II, who was granted permission by the

Anker's House Museum, St Mary and St Cuthbert's Church, Chester-le-Street.

King and the Bishop of Durham to build this fortified house. The castle is now an hotel but does retain one tradi-

The south-west tower of Lumley Castle, Chester-le-Street.

tional castle feature, the ghost of a white lady — Lily of Lumley — who is said to haunt the building.

Lambton Castle

LAMBTON Castle was built in the early 1800s on a site originally occupied by Harraton Hall, an Elizabethan mansion. This hall belonged to the Hedworth family who were united to the Lambtons by marriage. Lambton Castle was designed by fashionable country house architect of the time, Ignatius Bonomi, who, it is said, 'built castles for all tastes'. The buttresses carry no loads, the battlements are ornamental and the turrets serve no real purpose, but this castle is an impressive sight, set high above the River Wear in beautifully landscaped wooded grounds. The castle was the home of one of the most famous Lambtons, 'Radical Jack'. John George Lambton was Parliamentary representative for Durham and was created the first Earl of Durham in 1833. He was ambassador to Imperial Russia and recommended home rule for Canada, only to become its first Governor-General. He was such a popular figure that the famous Penshaw Monument was raised to him in 1844, funded by public subscription.

The Lambton family has been settled in County Durham since the 12th century; connected with them is the famous legend of the Lambton Worm:

Sometime before the Crusades, John, the young heir of Lambton, would spend his Sundays fishing instead of going to church. To the dismay of all, he would curse loud and long when he caught nothing.

One such day he was about to go home when he felt a mighty pull on his line, an intense struggle ensued but eventually he landed the catch. It was not a big fish, as he had hoped, but a strange worm-like creature of revolting appearance. He was so disgusted by this thing that he threw it into a nearby well, exclaiming that he had indeed 'caught the Devil himself'.

Young John, inspired by the anticipation of adventure, then went off to join the Crusades, and completely forgot about the worm. However, '*it grew and grew and grew an aaful size*', too big for the well. It slithered from the dark depths and found another home — a large rock in the middle of the river. The worm continued to grow and became the terror of the whole district. It would savagely devour anything that got in its way. Nothing was safe, it would eat sheep, lambs, calves and pigs and would even suck dry the milking cows to slake its awesome thirst but, worst of all, we are told, 'It would swally little bairns alive when they lay down to sleep'. The creature was an absolute abomination, indulging in foul gluttony, and after it had gorged itself would sleep and 'lap its tail ten times round Penshaw Hill'. The north side of the river was soon laid waste and barren, the people were in the cold grip of mortal fear. The worm crossed to the south side of the river to Lambton Hall, where the old Lord lived, lamenting the fact that his son had gone to fight in the Holy Land.

The steward of the Hall, a man of great experience, devised a plan which was to ease the situation. He filled a drinking trough with milk for the worm which it would consume on its

(opposite page)
Lambton Castle.

visits and return to its lair without causing further damage. The dreadful worm returned every day at the same time but its appetite was appeased with the milk of nine cows in the trough — if the contents were any less it would fly into a rage, lashing its tail, uprooting trees in the park. Many brave knights had come from far and wide to try to kill the dreadful monster but nearly all were killed, and those who escaped death, suffered severe injury. The few who had managed to cut the worm in half were thwarted by its ability to rejoin the severed halves! After seven long years Sir John returned from the Holy Wars but was desperately distressed to find his beloved lands laid desolate. He crossed the river to examine the beast. He was told of the fate of those who had previously tried to kill the worm so he decided to consult a soothsayer to find the solution. She told him that he was responsible for the foul creature that inflicted such misery on the area, therefore it was he who must kill the beast. She said that he must have his strongest suit of chainmail fitted with razor-sharp blades, and that he must fight the fearsome creature to the death on a rock in the middle of the river.

But, to ensure the outcome of the fight would be in his favour, he must take a solemn vow to slay the first living thing he would meet after killing the worm, or a curse would fall on the family — the next nine generations of Lambtons would not die in their beds.

'Bowld and brave' Sir John took up his position and waited for the worm to make its way towards the Hall. It came upon him in the middle of the river, barring its progress. It reared up to attack but Sir John struck it a mighty blow to the head. This only angered the beast and in fury it coiled itself around the brave knight and tried to crush him to death, but it only managed to give itself severe deep wounds on the blades on Sir John's armour — the river ran red with blood. The more the beast tried to crush the knight the more severe its wounds became. The foul beast weakened and Sir John hacked off its loathsome head with his trusty sword, its body was carried downstream on a foaming wave of water stained with its blood and, unable to join itself back together, the creature died.

Sir John gave a blast on his hunting horn to let his father know he was safe and that he should, as agreed, turn loose Sir John's favourite hound so that it could be slain to fulfil the vow. In his excitement the old man forgot and rushed out to meet his son. Young Lambton did not want to kill his father and blew his horn again.

This time his father remembered and sent out the dog. Sir John killed his favourite hound, hoping that this would fulfil the vow. Alas this was not to be and the next nine generations of Lambtons suffered untimely deaths.

It is interesting to note that Surtees, the respected Durham historian, during a visit to the Lambton estate in his younger days, was shown a stone trough and a 'piece of tough substance, resembling an extremely thick piece of bull's hide' said to be part of the worm's skin.

The estate is not open to the public, which is probably just as well — wandering in the thickly wooded grounds you can't help looking over your shoulder, just to keep an eye open for anything untoward lurking by the edge of the silent, deep river, or in the gloomy, dense undergrowth…

Beamish Museum

BEAMISH was the first regional open-air museum in England. It was the brainchild of Frank Atkinson who, as far back as 1952, organised the collection of everyday items relating to the history of County Durham. In 1974, his dream was realised when Beamish Museum was opened to the public.

The museum shows, by way of reconstruction, the industrial, social and domestic heritage of the county, giving visitors the opportunity to step back into living history. It vividly recreates life in northern England in the 18th and 19th centuries. Costumed staff welcome visitors to the turn-of-the-century town with shops, houses,

The museum's reconstruction of a Durham school.

stationers, sweet shop and sweet factory, garage, and by no means least, a working pub. There is a real 'drift mine' near the Colliery Village, with guided tours. The row of pit cottages, brought here and reconstructed as originally built, show what life was like for the pitmen and their families. Chapel and school are represented and there are traditional games to play in the playground. The nearby Railway Station has a signal box, engines, rolling stock and a goods yard. The Home Farm has

Pitmen's cottages and gardens, Beamish Museum.

Beamish Museum's Pockerley Manor Farm (left) and drift mine, (right).

a large farmhouse kitchen and dairy, as well as livestock and machinery. At Pockerley Manor Farm the accent is on the life of a yeoman farming family of nearly 200 years ago, including packhorses and a splendid heavy horse yard.

Original trams, buses and cars transport visitors around the site to complete the experience.

(below) Town scene, Beamish Museum.

Beamish is an established part of north-eastern life and visitors flock here from all over the world. It has won many major awards, proving it is a popular and successful way of preserving our past. It also provides, in huge measure, that valuable, intangible commodity — nostalgia.

Causey Arch, Tanfield

CAUSEY Arch is tucked away from the busy tourist routes which serve Britain's explorers. It is, however, a must for those who appreciate the

unique, as it is the oldest surviving railway bridge in the world, and, indeed, for 30 years it was the largest single-span bridge in Britain.

By the mid-1600s coal was being transported by horses pulling carts (Chaldron wagons) on wooden rails. As more mines were opened the railways were extended. A powerful group of local coal owners, known as the 'Grand Allies', demanded a new line to serve the pits near Tanfield. A massive embankment provided one route across the Causey Burn, and to provide another, a local master mason, Ralph Wood, was commissioned to build a bridge 350 yards upstream. Basing his construction on Roman engineering principles he achieved his masterpiece — a single span of a 100ft, with a deck

Causey Arch, near Tanfield (above), Chaldron wagon (left).

80ft above the burn. At the peak of its use, a staggering figure of 950 crossings a day has been calculated.

An underground fire in 1740 resulted in the closure of Tanfield Colliery and the need for the bridge diminished. By the 1780s it ceased to operate and in disuse became unsafe until it was restored by Durham County Council in 1981.

Tradition has it that Ralph Wood, concerned that an earlier wooden bridge had collapsed, and fearing that the same would happen to his stone bridge, leapt to his death from the parapet of the arch before it was completed. He need not have worried because the bridge was certainly built well ahead of its time and survives today as a unique monument to the engineering marvels of the Industrial Revolution.

Tanfield Railway

TANFIELD Railway is reputed to be the oldest existing railway in the world. It started life as a wooden waggonway with horse-drawn trucks at the dawn of the Industrial Revolution in 1725. The line was the largest transporter of coal in Britain during the 18th century. Eventually, in 1841, steam arrived on the railway in the form of stationary engines which hauled trucks by means of lengthy cables. The Tanfield line is unusual in that it was one of the few wooden lines in Britain that eventually became a part of the main line system. The first passenger service on this railway operated in 1842, establishing it as one of the first branch lines in Britain. In 1881, 156 years of horse operation and 40 years of the stationary steam engine winding operation came to an end with the introduction of the steam railway locomotive.

After the closure of many local collieries the line fell into disuse. However, in 1971, a few enthusiasts got together and, using the Marley Hill Engine Shed as a base, they began the daunt-

Tanfield Railway, and Marley Hill Engine Shed.

ing task of restoring steam locomotives to run once again in the north-east. The Tanfield Railway is still based in the Marley Hill Engine Shed — the oldest working steam engine shed in the world — and now has a vast collection of restored engines, rolling stock, and machinery from all over the world. Thanks to this dedicated band of enthusiasts, steam railways are still working where they began — in County Durham.

Shotley Bridge Swordmakers

WE tend to presume, as we look back into the history of our county, that each generation is simply the product of even earlier Britons, although in reality there have been infusions of foreign blood from across the water from time immemorial.

One exciting example of particular interest to County Durham folk is the swordmakers of Solingen, Germany, who came to Shotley Bridge late in the 17th century and made it the centre of England's swordmaking industry — as long as the wars of William III protracted the demand.

Why to Shotley Bridge? Many explanations have been offered. Some believe they were induced to come by a small consortium of English businessmen anxious to benefit from the growing armaments trade. Others say that due to acute rivalry between guildsmen over methods and patents in their homeland, they chose to emigrate with their secret formula for making the prized hollow blades. Then there was undoubtedly the escape-from-religious-persecution theory, too, as they were Lutherans.

Their route was apparently from Germany to Rotterdam, across to the port of Newcastle, up the Tyne and its tributary, the Derwent, to Shotley. There they would find the ideal circumstances to re-establish their trade: remoteness from competition, yet good supplies of iron ore for smelting, excellent fuel sources, the Derwent to power their mills, Gateshead gritstone for their grinding and the Tyne for transportation. Even the local spa water was, they found, especially suitable for tempering their steel.

Whatever the reason, these settlers developed their skills and jealously-guarded techniques into a prosperous

Site of swordmaker's home, Shotley Bridge.

and lucrative industry in the Derwent valley. Today virtually nothing remains to commemorate their activity although through intermarriage with the community, their descendants live on amongst us. Two public houses, the Crown and the Crossed Swords, have been combined to leave us the only tangible memento since the industry ceased early in the 19th century.

Even the stone houses they built in Wood Street, down by the river in the old part of the village, have recently been demolished, leaving only the evidence of the lower courses. However, we have on record one of the doorhead inscriptions carved in old German but translated here as follows:

'The blessing of the Lord makes rich without care, so long as you are industrious in your vocation and do what is required of you. 1691.'

A fine axiom in any language, in any century.

Derwentcote Steel Furnace

DERWENTCOTE Steel Furnace dates from about 1720 and was one of a number of steel manufacturing works along the banks of the River Derwent. This area, along with neighbouring Tyneside, produced nearly half of Britain's steel output in the 18th century. 'Newcastle Steel', as it became known, enjoyed an international reputation for excellent quality.

A new, advanced method of steel

Derwentcote Steel Furnace, near Ebchester.

production had been brought to the North-East from Germany by William Bartram and his sons towards the end of the 17th century. This process fused the carbon from charcoal with very pure iron at very high temperatures to form high quality steel, and it was this technology which operated at the Derwentcote Furnace. Iron bars were loaded into stone chests with charcoal dust packed around them, and the top was sealed with a layer of sand. These stone chests prevented the charcoal from being burned away and the steel from absorbing the impure sulphur fumes from the coal. The flames from the coal fire in the grate below roared up around the chests and its intense heat would be reflected from the brick vaulting.

One of these cementation firings would take about a week to complete, at a steady temperature of over 1,000 degrees centigrade. Then it would be ten days before the 'Blister Steel' — the product of the process — was cool enough to be unloaded. The bars would then be forged to even out their carbon content and to restore their malleability.

The advantage of

processing the iron would be that steel could be easily forged as well as hardened or softened. This meant that it was ideal for producing the very sharp and durable edges needed for cutting tools, scythes, sword blades and cutlery. Its flexibility also meant it could be used in the manufacture of springs and for similar applications.

By the 19th century cementation had been replaced by the crucible process, making steel much easier and cheaper to produce. Derwentcote Steel Furnace ceased production in the 1870s

Derwentcote Furnace.

Beehive Coke Ovens at Hedley Hill, Deerness Valley.

and soon fell into disrepair. Fortunately, in 1985 it was taken into the care of English Heritage and carefully restored. It remains today a unique example of the earliest and most complete steel-making furnace of the period, when Derwentside was at the centre of Britain's steel industry.

Hedley Hill Coke Ovens

COAL mined in south-west Durham was ideal for converting into coke, the fuel used in the new-fangled railway engines, because they had to 'consume their own smoke'! Later, from the 1840s onwards, the iron-making blast furnaces of Durham and Teesside with their voracious appetite for coke had to be supplied. To satisfy this enormous market, coke ovens were set up beside those collieries which had direct rail connections, such as at Hedley Hill.

The railway was opened in 1858 and the coke ovens shortly afterwards. They were built in long rows side by side and were shaped like the old circular, domed beehives, hence their name — 'Beehive Coke Ovens'. The ovens had an opening at the top for feeding in the coal, and an arched opening on one side for withdrawing the white-hot coke. This was pulled out with coke rakes on to a flat area, the 'bench', where it was quickly dowsed with water. The process was to burn coal with a restricted amount of air in order to cleanse it of its impurities and leave behind pure, unburned carbon. The ovens were charged with about four tons of coal to a depth of about 27ins (69cms) and lit. The tops were then sealed but small holes were left for air supply. The coal expanded under the heat and all the impurities, sulphur, and other noxious fumes billowed out from the top of the

The 12-arched, brick-built Hownsgill Viaduct.

oven. The whole process took about three days, and since this was staggered, ovens were being opened and recharged every hour of the day and night.

There were about 14,000 Beehive Coke Ovens in County Durham in 1877, producing over four million tons of coke. The fumes and stench would reach into everything — house, shop, school, church and chapel. The air improved when they were eventually replaced by By-product Recovery Ovens, the first of which were built at Crook in 1882. With these ovens all the fumes were led into washers and coolers to collect the profitable by-products, coal-tar, benzene, naphtha and so forth. Some collieries continued to produce coke in beehive ovens and therefore these were not destroyed and survive as examples of this early process.

Hownsgill Viaduct

ON THE course of the old Stanhope & Tyne Railway between Consett and Rowley is a magnificent example of Victorian railway engineering. Hownsgill Viaduct has no river or stream beneath, just a dry valley, or wind gap, which was an extreme handicap to the railway. Wagons had to be manoeuvred, one by one, on to a cradle at the top of the gorge. The cradle ran on an inclined track to the bottom where the wagon was manhandled for a short distance across the floor of the gorge and on to a similar cradle which climbed up the other side. These cradles were linked by ropes so that a descending one helped to haul up an ascending one.

In 1856 the railway company, Stockton & Darlington, sought tenders for a viaduct. The chosen engineer was just about to embark on an exciting career of bridge-building and to be knighted for his work by Queen Victoria but was to end his life in disgrace because of the collapse of his greatest achievement — The Tay Bridge. He was Thomas Bouch. He believed that instead of building bridges as large solid structures, offering a greater resistance to wind and gales they should be slender, allowing the wind to blow through, and, if possible, constructed from iron.

Here, at Hownsgill, he built in brick, using almost three million white (now off-white!) firebricks, made at the Pease Brickworks in Crook. He built 12 arches, each with a 50ft span, at a maximum height of 150ft above the gorge. Each pillar was given two recesses on their inner faces to lighten the loading, and two small delicate buttresses on their inner faces to strengthen the pillars. Like many bridges, Hownsgill, too, has a legend. There is reputed to be a cross in red brick to the memory of those men who died during its construction. Fortunately no one did die while it was being erected, but there is a cross, high up on the north face of the fifth pillar from the south, but it is X-shaped in pattern and is therefore not a memorial cross. The reason for its presence is unknown, but it is an intriguing mystery.

Thomas Raw — Border Reiver

ONE of the joys of rambling, is keeping an eye open for the unusual and a great joy is finding something unusual where least expected. Certainly not to be expected would be an inscribed tombstone set high in the gable end of a farmyard barn and yet this is awaiting the observant rambler at Steeley Farm, Satley. It commemorates an unusual man, Thomas Raw, who died in 1714.

Although he was ostensibly a farmer of Wharnley Burn, between Castleside and Allansford, he has since been alternatively described as outlaw, moss-trooper, free-booter and highwayman. Whichever be the most accurate, his lifestyle earned him the wrath of the church and he was excommunicated. Knowing he could not be buried in consecrated ground, he chose a plot on his own land, said to be where he had always been able to see anyone approaching, friend or foe. There in 1714 he was laid to rest, having died peacefully in his own bed despite his villainous life.

His son erected a tombstone over the grave and successive generations continued to farm Wharnley Burn, no doubt with great respect for their forebear's burial place because when the farm changed ownership a century and a half later, it seemed natural to remove their ancestor's tombstone, although there appears no record of his remains also being removed.

It is, however, on record that his

remains were exhumed in about 1930, the skeleton inspected and re-interred. But why? Evidence seems quite conclusive — he was no saint.

(left) Barn at Steeley Farm, (right) Roman Fort, near Lanchester.

Roman Aqueduct serving Lanchester Fort

LONGOVICIUM, as the Romans knew it, is to be found at the top of Cadger Bank. There is a convenient lay-by in which to park and walk back to view the very sparse remains of the perimeter wall which sadly encloses no visible traces, so much of the fort's masonry having been subsequently used as a readily available source of prepared building stone.

An interesting ancillary feature is the aqueduct which supplied the fort with water. The course of this can be traced, albeit only intermittently, as it cuts its way over the four miles from the dam which the Romans constructed near Dyke Nook Farm. This was strategically sited to collect water from two streams converging at that point. The fort's water supply was supplemented by a second dam, storing supplies gained from springs prevalent in the area slightly westward of the Dyke Nook Dam but this dam seems to have been destroyed.

Perhaps the most obvious stretch of the aqueduct visible today is the section alongside the road (B6296) from Hollinside Terrace to Colepike Hall.

In looking back over this length of Roman civil engineering and through perhaps 18 centuries of time, the immensity of their task may not be wholly realised. The terrain was almost total wilderness, their equipment primitive and they were in hostile country, but the practical genius, discipline and determination of the Roman invaders knew no bounds and fortunately for us, laid the foundations of our civilisation.

Line of the Roman aqueduct between Hollinside Terrace and Colepike Hall.

Langley Hall, Witton Gilbert

HIDDEN away in dense woodland, two miles west of Witton Gilbert, is an impressive ruin of a fortified manor house built in the early 16th century by Henry, Lord Scrope of Bolton, York-

The now derelict Langley Hall.

shire. This stronghold was built around three sides of a square courtyard and was protected by a moat on two sides and the Langley Burn to the south.

Now in a dangerously ruinous condition, despite standing three storeys on the west wing, the gaunt shell provides ample evidence of the original layout and construction. The overwhelming temptation is to sit down on a moss-cushioned block of stone, in the midst of it all, to interpret the scene; to mentally eliminate the mature trees which have invaded this once magnificent house, now open to the sky; to summon sufficient strength to lift that massive window head to complete at least one of the stark openings; to scramble through the tumbled masonry and rescue the moulded stone door jamb, carved with heraldic shield, so completing the courtyard entrance to the west wing's hall.

Eventually abandoned in the mid-18th century, it has crumbled into its present state over these last 250 years. Not a fragment of medieval timberwork survives to indicate the wonderful ceilings or roof structures; not a ceramic tile lies exposed to reveal the interior floor decoration.

To complete the setting it is necessary to mentally populate the original household with family and servants dressed in the costume of Tudor times. But thankfully the continuing bird song can still provide nature's own orchestral backcloth, as it has done through the centuries.

Muggleswick Grange

ON THE Durham-Northumberland border where the River Derwent marks the boundary are the remote remains of the Muggleswick Grange. Off the beaten track it may be, but it is accessible to the public by courtesy of Grange Farm whose approach road leads to this impressive ruin, on the edge of their farmyard.

Surprisingly, this 13th-century gable survives to its full height, supported by two substantial corner towers. Originally it was part of the Prior's Grange, and it would now seem debatable whether this was the east gable of their manor house or their chapel. Its architecture is certainly indicative of its importance within the complex. Curiously, a traceried window, of a later period, has been walled up both internally and externally, to a height whereby its former total glory can only be conjectured. Internally a fireplace has been inserted immediately below the original window opening.

This Grange (a manor house integral with a farm) would be one of many covering the county, which the Benedictine priors of Durham built to provide lodgings for themselves and their entourage when on their travels, or for holidays and hunting parties. Hugh de Darlington, prior from 1258-72 and again from 1286-90, created the hunting park here and built the Grange — but the estate had been in the hands of the priors since before 1185 when it was mentioned in the *Boldon Book*.

The area of enclosed parkland was three miles by two miles and considered an important hunting park although it was nowhere near as extensive as the Bishop's Hunting Park in Weardale. The farm would possibly only produce corn for sale and consumption.

Nearby stands the present church which, strangely, has no known dedication. A small and simple structure, it was a rebuilding of 1728 with subsequent restorations. No doubt it consists of much of the earlier masonry robbed from the ruins of the original buildings, evidence of which must lie below ground, awaiting future investigation.

Muggleswick Grange.

Waskerley and the Weardale & Derwent Junction Railway

IN 1831 William Wallis of Westoe conceived the idea of building a waggonway to link Stanhope, in Weardale, with the River Tyne. The plentiful supply of limestone from the quarries above Stanhope, together with the lead from the smelters of Stanhope and Rookhope, provided the incentive.

Thirty-four miles of waggonway were planned and, to avoid what they assumed would be considerable opposition to the project, the promoters of the Stanhope & Tyne Railway deliberately decided not to seek Parliamentary powers.

They relied instead on a series of private negotiations for a succession of 'way-leaves', or rights of way, rented from the adjoining landowners. The first sums agreed were reasonable, the average fee at the western end of the line was as little as £25 per mile per year. Unfortunately, the nearer the negotiations got to South Shields, the more apparent the promoters' plan became and they were forced to agree much higher rates, in some cases in excess of £300.

Waskerley engine shed and track bed (left), Stockton & Darlington (S&D) trackside marker (right).

The building of the line began in 1832, but because of the landscape and the contours of the area it was not opened until 15 May 1834. Start-up costs and running expenses were crippling and the Stanhope & Tyne Railway was wound up in 1840 with debts of £300,000.

The Stockton & Darlington Railway took over the line and was in operation, under the name of the Weardale & Derwent Junction Railway, by 1845. The same year it was decided to develop Waskerley as a railway centre and its rapid growth began. A locomotive depot was established and in 1846 the engine shed was opened. Sidings were laid down and offices and stores were built. The village expanded to house the workers and eventually it had a church,

The Waskerley Way follows the old trackbed.

a chapel and a school. A wagon repair shop was set up and by 1847 the importance of the depot increased again when major changes to the routes allowed more locomotives to work the line. By 1854 the traffic requirements were so great that an additional engine shed was built.

Waskerley became a well-known railway village, renowned for the toughness of its railwaymen — and no wonder considering the wild, bleak, moorland terrain in which they lived.

For many years the line continued to provide a successful freight and passenger service which gradually settled down to four trains a day in either direction. Passenger services at the station stopped on 1 May 1939 but Waskerley continued as a goods station until 2 August 1965. The line was finally closed to traffic on 29 April 1968.

Things have changed dramatically at Waskerley and now the only sounds are the whistle of the wind and the call of the curlew, although it is easy to imagine the ghosts of those old railwaymen pursuing their phantom tasks.

Western County Durham: Weardale

Auckland Castle

UNTIL recently, the privilege of viewing the interior of the Bishop of Durham's princely residence was restricted to one open-day each year. The public's response on these occasions was some indication of the regard in which the building was held by those who could otherwise only gaze in wonderment at its majestic exterior as they walked through the Bishop's Park.

The impressive Gothic Gatehouse, seen from the market square, draws the visitor to walk along the drive towards the extensive parkland where the bishop's herd of fallow deer once roamed. On the left is an unusual architectural feature, a high screen of worked stone and wrought iron, which seems to protect the Bishop's Palace from the outside world. It is penetrated by a recessed, central, triple archway which frames an excellent view of the range of buildings which comprise the palace, built over the centuries and representing many periods of architecture.

Grand though it is, it was only one of a number of residences within the county, although today it is the only survivor. Durham Castle was the bishop's town residence but in the days of slow progress over unmetalled roads, he could use the castle or manor house most conveniently located. One of his castles, overlooking the River Tees at Stockton, would be ideal as a port of arrival and departure when travelling to London in those early days.

The park at Auckland provided for

The castle gateway (left) and chapel's ceiling (right).

89

the bishops' sporting recreation in the form of hunting, although they had alternative hunting parks in Weardale. At Auckland, Bishop Richard Trevor (1752-71) built a deer house to give winter protection to the animals and suitable accommodation for hunting parties to rest and celebrate their successes.

For hundreds of years Auckland has been the residence of a succession of bishops. Until 1836 they were aptly called Prince Bishops, rich and powerful men who combined the roles of church leaders, defenders of their territory, and politicians. Their territory was centred upon the county of Durham, and was known as the Palatinate, the bishops having received royal sanction to raise their own armies, administer their own courts, and even mint their own coinage. Many of these powerful men ranked in income with the richer peers of the realm and were

thus able to leave their mark on the structure of the building in one way or another.

So it is for its architectural features that the castle is considered to be most interesting. The splendid St Peter's Chapel was built originally as a 12th-century banqueting hall, but later transformed by Bishop John Cosin (1660-71). He will be forever renowned for his remarkable architectural taste, especially for fine carved woodwork.

The long Entrance Hall, thought to be part of the original manor building, has lost its high timbered roof, masked by a false ceiling, which was introduced by architect James Wyatt under the direction of Bishop Shute Barrington (1791-1826). He, perhaps more than any other bishop, transformed the castle interior, in the belief that architectural decoration should be 'co-ordinated'.

At the far end of the Entrance Hall,

Auckland Castle, Bishop Auckland.

Auckland Castle's magnificent entrance hall.

the elegant double staircase leads to the State Rooms. The octagonal Ante-Room and the Throne Room were originally built as one, to be the Common Room, by Bishop Anthony Bek (1283-1311). They display numerous portraits of former bishops which contrast with the beautifully vaulted false ceilings erected by Wyatt. Indeed this wonder-

ful collection of paintings helps us to relive the history of our county.

The Long Dining Room, aptly named from its 60ft length, was added by Bishop Cuthbert Tunstall (1530-61) but has since had the ceiling and east window changed by Bishops Trevor and Barrington. The major art collection displayed in the Long Dining Room is of special interest: it comprises a series of oil paintings by the Spanish artist Francisco de Zurbaran (1598-1664) of Jacob and 11 of his 12 sons. These 8ft-high paintings which dominate the room, were bought by Bishop Trevor, a keen art collector, in 1756 for £125 5s 0d.

He then completed the series by paying £22 6s 0d to have a copy made of Benjamin, the son who had somehow escaped the collection. The value of the collection is now probably inestimable. We are indeed fortunate that it was retained when so much of the contents of the palace was sold in the 1930s.

Of the State Rooms open to the public there remains only the beautiful King Charles Room, so named because Charles I used it as a bedroom on his journeys to Scotland. It has since been re-designed as a dining room and is used as such by the bishop on special occasions.

The Bishop's Palace is now open to the public on a regular basis, allowing us more opportunity to enrich our knowledge of the County Palatine of Durham.

The deerhouse in Auckland Park.

Church of St Andrew's Auckland

ST ANDREW'S Auckland is the biggest parish church in County Durham. It is well situated on a small hill overlooking the edge of the town. The presence of a Saxon stone cross within the church suggests that this hill may well have been the centre of an 8th-century Christian community. The cross, or possibly a small prayer house, would have stood on the site. No part of the pre-Conquest church survives. The church we see today belongs almost entirely to the 13th century with several additions from later centuries incorporated into its fabric. The tower was originally topped by a wooden spire sheathed in lead but this was replaced by the crenellated top storey of the tower in 1416.

The church owes its size to being originally a collegiate church. This would be staffed by a dean and canons who were expected to say mass in due form. As a religious community they were required to live in the college buildings and to pray for the souls of the local population whilst demonstrating a fine example of Christian life. Bishop Auckland was a rich parish and its income was used to support members of the bishop's staff. The bishops were anxious to provide themselves with an establishment to rival the support which the Priors of Durham enjoyed from the Cathedral Chapter. Auckland seemed to be a natural choice for such a foundation since the bishops had already built a hunting lodge here which had become their favourite residence.

It is uncertain just when St Andrew's was constituted as a collegiate church but it is possible that some sort of

Durham's largest parish church — St Andrew's, Bishop Auckland.

establishment of dean and prebendaries existed here from the time of Bishop William of Carileph. Its beginning is sometimes ascribed to Bishop Anthony Bek, although evidence suggests that he was not the original founder and, in fact, it was he who reorganised it in 1292. His deed of foundation supports this theory by making mention of the prior existence of a collegiate establishment, although this does seem to have been in complete disarray. Bek re-formed the college and increased its resources and provided land so that accommodation could be built for the canons. However, despite his good intentions Bishop Bek proved just as willing as previous bishops to use the revenue of the church to provide his staff with levels of income suitable to their positions.

It was during the reign of Bishop Laurence Booth, between 1457 and 1476, that the collegiate establishment was transferred to the Bishop's Palace. At the Reformation the property of all collegiate churches was vested in the Crown and at Bishop Auckland the former collegiate establishment was replaced by a vicar and three curates.

Despite many difficulties over the years, St Andrew's has still seen the tradition of worship carried on over the centuries by many generations of Christians.

Newton Cap Viaduct, Bishop Auckland

IT IS difficult not to notice the impressive Newton Cap Viaduct on the edge of Bishop Auckland. It carries the A689 road to Crook across the Wear valley on an 11-arch span at a height of over 100ft.

The bridge was originally a railway viaduct. Building started in 1854 but the bridge was not opened until 1 April 1857 because of problems with the foundations which eventually had to be sunk 20ft below the riverbed. The new line, opened for mineral traffic, was part of the Bishop Auckland Branch Contract for the North Eastern Railway. The viaduct continued in use for 111 years up to 1968 when the line closed. In 1972 the viaduct was acquired by Durham County Council who, in 1974, converted it to a footway as part of a network of country paths. Durham County Council was one of the first councils in England to realise the value of opening its disused railway trackbeds as country walks.

The £4.25 million conversion of Newton Cap was begun in September 1993 and was opened to traffic in July 1995, providing a more satisfactory link with the other side of the valley than the old bridge far below, built by Bishop Skirlaw in the 14th century. With the conversion of the viaduct to a road bridge it was found necessary to widen the deck to accommodate the road and two footpaths. This had to be done without a big increase in weight.

Durham County Council and Bullen Consultants devised a special design for the scheme, thought to be novel in this type of work. A reinforced concrete saddle-deck slab with pre-cast concrete parapets was laid across the length of the viaduct — effectively forming a roof over the existing stone-work. This was, essentially a repetition of the original hollow construction and resulted in a mere 2 per cent increase in total weight.

Because of its exposed position, the

Newton Cap Viaduct, Bishop Auckland.

viaduct is subject to very strong winds, so an anemometer and wind vane were installed on the bridge, connected to the weather centre by a dial-up telephone line. This would allow wind-strength alerts to be issued to the police and the County Council. It is also possible for the wind strength to be read directly by the police, allowing them to set the variable message signs remotely, or locally, to divert high-sided vehicles.

The award-winning conversion of Newton Cap Viaduct from rail to road use is thought to be the first of its kind in the country. It is a wonderful blend of Victorian and 20th-century Elizabethan talents and richly deserves to be recognised as a milestone in civil engineering.

Binchester Roman Fort

LATE in the first century, as the conquering Romans swept resolutely northward through our county, hur-riedly constructing their marching camps along the way, they selected strategic sites for their permanent bases or forts. It was always necessary to position a fort to defend river crossings on the routes they were establishing. This route through what eventually would be County Durham was to become known as Dere Street and would eventually run from York towards the Wall and beyond to the Firth of Forth.

Binchester was one such fort on Dere Street. The Romans called it Vinovia but since as early as 1183 it has been recorded as Binchester, or more precisely, Bynchestre. Dere Street had entered the county at Piercebridge, where it crossed the River Tees. Twelve miles further north, where its route crossed the River Wear, near Bishop Auckland, it was essential to build another fort. The elevated plateau which nature offered 100ft above the river, served the Roman builders ideally for their initial fort and subsequent

garrison town, the greater part of which still lies beneath the fields awaiting the archaeologist.

Although the site was selectively excavated late in the 19th century, at the instigation of enthusiastic archaeologist R.E.Hooppell, Rector of Byers Green, and through the generosity of local benefactor John Proud, only the commanding officer's bath house and a portion of the adjacent Dere Street are exposed today for visitors who are, however, rewarded with the sight of the finest Roman military bath house in Britain. It is under cover and thoroughly explained on information boards. Indeed in summertime, under the heat of the glazed roof, it is not difficult to re-live the hot baths environment.

The true extent of the buried town is difficult to ascertain because over the centuries nature has partially destroyed the fort even more effectively than hundreds of years of stone-robbers. As the Roman Empire declined, all their forces were withdrawn from Britain and the abandoned town became little more than a quarry of ready-prepared building stone. Gradually the River Wear has changed course, encroaching ever nearer to Vinovia. The western side of the town has slipped and been continuously washed away so that many of the buildings fronting on to the west side of Dere Street have been lost along with the west rampart.

If, however, Dere Street ran centrally through the fort, the position of the remaining ramparts would seem to suggest an area for the fort alone of approximately eight acres. With the total area of the surrounding town comprising civilian settlement, parade grounds and cemeteries, the area for potential excavation at Binchester is considerable and who knows what treasures may lie undiscovered beneath the turf on this intriguing site?

Hypocausted bath house, once for the exclusive use of the Roman commanding officer.

(opposite page) Archaeological excavation of Binchester Roman Fort.

Escomb Saxon Church, Bishop Auckland.

The Saxon Church, Escomb

IT SEEMS we have the fall of the Roman Empire and the consequent withdrawal of their forces from Britain in 410 AD to thank for one of the county's architectural gems, the Saxon church at Escomb, near Bishop Auckland.

Generally the Saxons built in wood and the church here would not have survived had it not been built of the stone which they transported from the nearby long-deserted Roman fort of Vinovia, or Binchester as it is now known.

Although its earliest years are unrecorded and there is no known dedication, the church was almost certainly built on an established site — as the circular-mounded perimeter wall suggests — and may well have succeeded an ear-

lier wooden structure when missionaries converted the Saxons to Christianity. In fact there have been relics of Christian worship discovered at Binchester Fort, indicating a certain degree of conversion to Christianity before the Romans' departure.

Much, if not all of the building material was brought from Binchester and undoubtedly Roman building technique was admired and adopted in the new work. The Romans had brought their stone-building expertise to Britain and the masonry of their deserted fort had stood for over 200 years until it attracted the attention of the Saxon builders.

Apart from the re-use of Roman walling material, there are a number of interesting features to be found both within and without. These are well indicated by information boards distributed about the church. The most impressive item is the tall, narrow chancel arch which has surely seen prior use at Binchester. There are two sundials on the south wall, one of which is Saxon and is believed to be the earliest example, still in its original position, to be found in Britain.

After surviving basically as built, except for the 12th-century addition of a south porch and a bell cote on the western gable, the fabric remains as a splendid example of the bold, sombre structures of the period and its simple internal beauty is preserved as an exquisite architectural relic, claimed to be without equal. Thankfully, it is a rare example of the Victorians missing an opportunity 'to extend and beautify'.

In 1863 the church suffered the ignominy of being relegated to the status of a mere chapel when it was replaced with a fine new building in the Early English style. This was erected half a mile away on the southern edge of the village and dedicated to St John. The old church had become quite dilapidated and the churchyard, tightly surrounded by the village, had been over-buried for centuries. Initially, occasional services were held there but it soon became a mere antiquity and gradually, a roofless ruin.

The timely recognition of the noted archaeologist, R.E.Hooppell, Rector of Byers Green, and later, the enthusiasm and determination of Thomas Lord, Vicar of Escomb, initiated great public support and the old church was restored and re-opened in 1880.

However, the Victorian church continued in use as the parish church until the 1960s when the Saxon church was fully furnished for regular worship, and finally, in 1970, it was restored to its

The Anglo-Saxon sundial at Escomb Church.

former status as parish church. This assured the future for the county's Saxon architectural treasure and sealed the fate of its successor which was demolished in 1971, leaving a ghostly space in the new churchyard among the monuments erected to the villagers who have been proud to worship in the churches of Escomb.

Devil's Stones, Crook

THE Devil's Stones, now landscaped into the green in Crook Market Place, have prompted many explanations and much speculation. Actually they were brought to their present position from nearby Dowfield Hill. They are thought to be glacial erratics, deposited there during the last Ice Age (8000 BC) and geologists tell us they originated from where we now know as Borrowdale, in the Lake District.

It is quite easy to understand how superstition evolved around these huge boulders, transported by superhuman force. No wonder the old belief was that they had been carried to the top of Dowfield Hill and dropped by the Devil himself.

Local children, playing on the hill, used to run around the stones three

The Devil's Stones, situated in Crook Market Place.

times to placate 'Old Nick'. Their elders were caught up in the superstition too; local quarry workers playing 'pitch and toss' on the hill would seek the blessing of the stones before enjoying their illegal gambling.

Who really knows the truth? Might it be just as well if YOU walk three times round the stones when you're next in Crook?

Memorial to the Revd John Ducket, Martyr

AFTER the effort of climbing Redgate Bank, which rises steeply from Wolsingham, in the direction of Tow Law, it is wise to pause awhile and recover breath.

The memorial cross to the Revd John Ducket.

Look southward and marvel at the panorama over Wolsingham and beyond. Look northward and read the inscription on a monu-

ment raised on the bank side. It mentally transports us back in time to this place in July 1644 when a troop of Cromwell's Parliamentary soldiers arrested a young Catholic priest together with his two lay companions, with whom he secretly lodged at Durham.

It was late evening and Father John Ducket was returning from christening two infants up the dale. Although he was disguised to conceal his true identity, it was clear someone had betrayed him. His possession of holy oils and the *Rituale Romanum,* together with other accoutrements of his calling, left no room for denial.

He was taken to Sunderland and imprisoned there, along with his two companions, but they were later released, luckily avoiding the death penalty for harbouring Catholic priests. Father Ducket was then shipped to London and committed to Newgate Prison, awaiting the next sessions, during which time he prepared himself to meet his Lord and Master, a joy he had always anticipated.

Born near Sedbergh in 1613, he had descended from staunch Catholic ancestry and at the age of 17 he was sent to the English College of Douai, in France, to complete his English education. There he was an outstanding pupil and eventually returned to England as an ordained priest in 1643, although necessarily landing incognito, as Queen Elizabeth had decreed it high treason for an Englishman, ordained abroad, to return to this country.

He immediately headed north and made his base in Durham, from where he selflessly served his scattered flock of recusants, regardless of the danger, evangelising, celebrating masses and administering the sacraments up to the very day of his capture.

Whilst his sentence now seems severe and barbaric, it was then commonplace and all knew the risks they took in defending their inherent faith since Henry VIII broke with the Church of Rome.

'You shall be placed on a wicker hurdle, and dragged to Tyburn, where you shall be half hanged with a rope, and when you are half dead, your bowels and heart shall be taken out and your body divided into four parts, which parts shall be taken to Newgate and exposed in some place appointed by His Majesty.'

But turn and look southward again, over sleepy Wolsingham. Thankfully, over the centuries, such barbarism has gradually changed, through stages of bigotry, tolerance and now ecumenism.

The work of Douai College continues, although since the French Revolution, it is now situated on English soil, at Ushaw College, near Durham. No doubt familiar ground to John Ducket on his clandestine journeys, to Flass Hall, Colepike and Minsteracres.

Whitfield House, Wolsingham

WHITFIELD House, in the main street of Wolsingham, was built about 1700. In keeping with the fashion of the time it boasts a magnificent parapet which hides the roof and accentuates the height of the three-storey front elevation.

The house is regarded as being of great architectural importance and as a

The listed Whitfield House, Wolsingham.

consequence, is a listed building, which protects it from extension, alteration or demolition without specific permission.

The evergreen trees in the front garden are holm oaks, natives of the Mediterranean, and are the only examples in County Durham.

Even though the building does have more in common with the town houses of the period, it still lends a certain amount of character and dignity to this dales market town.

Lime Kilns, White Kirkley

QUARRYING was a huge industry in Weardale during the Industrial Revolution and the area around Frosterley was worked extensively. The Bishop Auckland & Wear Valley Railway opened up a line in the dale in 1847 to make transportation of the stone easier by connecting with the historic Stockton & Darlington Railway. Enormous amounts of 'Mountain Limestone', as they called it, were quarried and burned to provide quicklime for industry and agriculture. Vast quantities were transported south to feed the blast furnaces of industrial Teesmouth and for use on the rolling agricultural land of North Yorkshire and Lower Teesdale.

The railway company built a series of lime kilns in the area and a lengthy,

The Lime Kilns at White Kirkley.

— the famous Frosterley Marble. This black, heavily fossilised limestone has been used as a decorative material in churches since medieval times. In County Durham its most famous use is, of course, in Durham Cathedral. Sawn and beautifully polished it produced the exquisite marble pillars of the Chapel Of The Nine Altars.

brick-built range still stands at White Kirkley.

The top part of these kilns would be filled with limestone and the base would be packed with alternate layers of coal and wood. Once ignited, it was a lengthy operation: the kilns would burn slowly for several weeks until the process was completed.

St Thomas's Church, Stanhope.

The quarries around Frosterley also produced another variety of limestone

St Thomas's Church, Stanhope

ST THOMAS'S Church, Stanhope, was built about 1200 AD and was one of the richest in County Durham. This was because at that time its parish was the biggest in England, covering an area of over 61,000 acres. The huge area, combined with the fact that Weardale had a large number of prosperous lead mines

reminder of the town's market which was held from 1421 until the mid-19th century.

Set into the wall of the churchyard is a fossilised tree stump, calculated to be over 250 million years old. It was discovered in a ganister quarry near Edmundbyers and was brought to Stanhope by Mr J.G.Beaston in 1962. This fossilised tree is a remarkable and fortunate exhibit. If it had just been carbonised, like most ancient trees it may well have been burnt as coal.

The Fossil Tree, Stanhope.

providing the usual tithe of ore mined, ensured a large income for the incumbent. This was a very attractive proposition and resulted in the rectorship of Stanhope being held, in many instances, by a non-resident bishop. Tunstall, Thurlow, Keen, Philpotts and Butler were all rectors at Stanhope. It was during his time at Stanhope that Joseph Butler wrote his famous *Analogy of Religion*, which is still considered a major source of reference

Part of the town's original market cross is on display in the churchyard, a

Stanhope Old Hall

STANHOPE Old Hall stands at the western edge of the market town on a small rise known as 'Dilly Hill'. The building was originally a fortified manor house but is now a comfortable hotel.

The first recorded occupancy of the building was in 1135 and for hundreds of years it was the seat of the powerful

The haunted Stanhope Old Hall.

Featherstonhaughs of Weardale. The house remained in the family until 1704 when the last male heir was killed in Austria, while serving with the Duke of Marlborough. Subsequently the Hall became a hunting lodge for the mighty Prince Bishops of Durham, being conveniently situated at the edge of their huge Upper Weardale hunting park.

The hall is reputed to be haunted and there are tales of many strange happenings associated with it. One such story tells of a betrothal celebration which took place many years ago. Late in the evening, in the main banqueting hall, the revelry was at its height when, suddenly, for no reason, every light in the place was extinguished, plunging the merrymakers into total darkness. During this unforeseen circumstance the couple vanished. After a lengthy search when the light had been restored, the couple could still not be found and everyone assumed they had slipped away to escape all the pomp and ceremony of the impending wedding.

However, many years later, the floor of the banqueting hall was in need of repair and several floorboards were removed. To the horror of the workmen, two human skeletons were discovered, lying hand in hand.

An eerie, unsettling tale, providing much food for thought.

Stanhope Police Station and Courthouse

STANHOPE Police Station and Courthouse was built in 1870 during the time that Durham's second Chief Constable was in office. Lieutenant-Colonel George Francis White had no previous police experience but had a distinguished military career. He had been second-in-command of the 31st Regiment and had served in four general actions in the Sikh War of 1845 and was awarded the campaign medal and clasp. He reorganised the Durham force and increased its manpower. By 1865, policing demands had increased dramatically and it was decided that the districts of Stanhope and Wolsingham should be separated from the district of Bishop Auckland.

Thus Stanhope got its own police station and courthouse. From its opening right up to 1946, when it was closed temporarily for refurbishment, it was staffed by one superintendent, three or four sergeants and about ten constables. Also staffing the station was an 'additional constable'. This was an officer who would be solely concerned with policing a major local industry, in the case of Stanhope, quarrying. Consequently part of their salary would be paid by the industry enjoying their services.

The station and courthouse are constructed of local stone. Quarrying was a huge industry around Stanhope in the late 1800s, so there would have been no shortage of raw material.

On the re-opening of the station, fewer policemen were needed because the station was merged with the Consett division and the force was making more use of motor vehicles, as opposed to bicycles.

Soon after occupying their new premises in Stanhope, the members of the local force were into immediate action. In 1870 it is recorded that an epidemic of typhus was raging in the dale — this and smallpox were com-

The Police Station and Courthouse.

mon in the area at that time — and although it wasn't directly a police matter, it still caused them many problems. A recently qualified young doctor, John Grey, who worked tirelessly during the epidemic, was to become police surgeon at Stanhope.

On 17 March 1871 two significant earthquake shocks shook Weardale, one at 6am and another at 11.30am, and, although these were felt throughout the county they were strongest in Weardale. As well as natural phenomena, the police also had to cope with civil unrest. In 1872 over 2,000 miners had to be controlled at an industrial meeting in the dale. Criminal law had to be upheld, of course, and a fight between Joseph Wearmouth and William Featherstone is recorded with a tragic outcome, when Wearmouth stabbed Featherstone in the abdomen with a clasp-knife. In the same year there were problems when sheep and cattle were struck by lightning in a dreadful storm.

Naturally, some of the things that the Stanhope force had to look out for in the 1800s are still a problem today, and it is on record that William Walton was fined £20 for taking grouse before the 12 August. A stiff fine for those days, perhaps, but one which reflects contemporary opinion of the severity of the crime.

Quarrying, of course, was responsible for another police activity: the examination and inspection of explosives, which, due to the size of the operations around the town, must have been a major occupation. Also, in one quarter alone it was reported that 57 stray dogs were seized but only 14 were claimed by their owners. This must have also been a great problem because of the number of sheep-worrying cases reported. Commendations and awards for good service were also given. For example, one officer was awarded 20 shillings *'for pluck and promptitude displayed in endeavouring to stop two runaway horses'.*

In the early days brawn was the chief requirement for a policeman serving in the dale and good manhandlers were preferred to those displaying more genteel qualities. The steps to promotion were governed by the number of convictions obtained — even to the point

*View into
Rookhope Valley,
from the ruined
railway cottages
at Bolt's Law.*

section. This incline was 1 mile 128 yards long with gradients of 1 in 12, 1 in 21 and 1 in 32 plus a short length at 1 in 10, but the average was 1 in 14. In 1919 a new engine house was built and the old engine was replaced with an improved 50hp model that could run four or six wagons at a time. These improvements, together with modifications to the sidings came to the princely sum of £4,046 5s 10d, the equivalent of over £500,000 at today's prices.

Bolts Law Incline

CHARLES Attwood formed the Weardale Iron Company in 1845 to exploit the iron ore resources of the dale. The company was so successful that it built a private mineral line from the large ironstone quarries near Westgate to connect with the Weardale & Derwent Junction Railway at Parkhead, above Stanhope.

The most spectacular section was, perhaps, the five and a half miles from Rookhope to Parkhead. It reached an altitude of 1,670 ft — the highest standard gauge railway in England — and also included what was believed to be the steepest railway incline in England.

Because of its great altitude, the section from Bolts Law to Parkhead suffered traffic disruption every winter. In

1883 the *Durham Advertiser* reported, '*The railway between Parkhead and Bolts Law, along which is carried the Upper Weardale ironstone and limestone, was blocked with snow on the Wednesday forenoon so that the snow-*

*Engine house
remains of the
Weardale Iron
Company.*

length and climbed over 500ft in height. The trucks were hauled by cables worked by a huge stationary steam engine at Redgate Head. The railway continued in use until 1923, after when the only traffic was wagons hauled by horses with supplies for the lead mines around Rookhope. It was finally closed about 1940 and the rails lifted in 1943.

The remains of the engine house, locomotive shed and the row of railway cottages are now in a ruinous condition but their silence seems to evoke an impression of the magnitude of this 19th-century feat of railway engineering.

Winding house remains and trackbed at Bolts Law.

plough had to be brought into requisition. The snow in some of the cuttings was 3ft to 6ft deep.' This was not unusual for a dales winter, of course — but the day in question was 11 May!

Bolts Law incline was over a mile in

Swinhope Head House

SWINHOPE Head House was a packhorse inn dating from the 17th century when only this mode of transport enabled the development of lead mining in the North Pennines.

As many as 25 dales ponies, tied together, would plod in single file along this route over Swinhope Head between Newbiggin in Teesdale and Westgate in

Bolts Law Incline, near Rookhope.

The 17th-century Swinhope Head House.

The remains of the chimney arch, Rookhope.

ed at the packhorse inns overnight and would be foddered and stabled while their drivers would enjoy the landlord's table and simple accommodation.

There were many such licensed inns in the county but in these remote areas they succumbed to the advent of railways and mechanised transport. This example is now used as a farm building but two packhorse inns surviving to this day at Stanhope and Burnopfield could also have been on this ancient network of routes.

Weardale. They would carry ore to the smelt mills and, eventually, the processed lead to the River Tyne for shipment to London. These dales ponies were dependable for a hard day's work and were larger than supposed, standing at about 14 hands. They were capable of carrying loads in excess of 440lbs over rough country, sometimes covering over 250 miles in a week. They rest-

Rookhope Smelt Mill Chimney Arch

DURING the Industrial Revolution, Rookhope was an important lead mining centre — the village even boasted its own smelt mill. The first mill at Rookhope was built in 1752 but it was rebuilt in 1884 after being described as both '*antiquated*' and '*inefficient*'. The new mill had

The early-17th-century Westernhopeburn Farm.

five ore hearths, a slag hearth, a refining hearth, and a roasting furnace. In the early days peat was burned for fuel. The cutting took place in May and June and was a huge operation. It would take over 100 men and women and 24 horses and carts to cut, carry and stack a year's supply for the mill. Later, a mixture of peat and coal was used in the hearths but mills fitted with reverberating furnaces used only coal.

The flue extended 2,548 yards in a north-westerly direction up Redburn Common to a height of 1,829ft where it belched out its noxious fumes into the clean moorland air — even today this area is devoid of vegetation. Along the length of this surface tunnel, a series of condenser chambers with manholes were constructed. The enormous length of the chimney not only created a huge draught to keep the smelters burning fiercely but also acted as a depository for particles of lead and silver that were a by-product of the process.

Understandably, the sweep's job was very important to the profitability of the company and at weekends he would bring in teams of young boys to retrieve the valuable deposits which otherwise would have been lost.

The single remaining chimney arch of the Rookhope Smelt Mill stands as a poignant reminder of a once prosperous industry, long since abandoned.

Westernhopeburn Farm

WESTERNHOPEBURN Farm is situated on the 'back road' that runs from Stanhope to Daddry Shield on the south side of the river. It dates from 1606 and its exterior has changed little since it was built. The long two-storeyed house has symmetrically arranged mullioned windows under hood moulds. The steep stone slate roof is typical of the era. It is such a pity that many of these wonderful roofs have been lost to the dale; the problem is, however, that the cost of the timbers to support such a weighty construction, when it comes to replacement, is prohibitive. The garden is typical of the dales, a pleasing harmony of shrubs, flowers and stone.

The farm was once part of the vast estate belonging to the Hildyards who were a prominent dales family for over 500 years. They lived in the nearby Horsley Hall and the last of their line was E.J.W.Hildyard, the well-known local archaeologist. His six-volume work on his finds and discoveries in Weardale is still considered a notable source of information.

High Mill, Westgate

HIGH Mill is now a private home but once ground corn for the inhabitants of Westgate and surrounding parts in an age when all communities had to be self-sufficient. Once there were two cornmills in the village, hand-operated 'querns', but production from these was low and they were replaced by the water-driven variety when the land was more extensively farmed and more corn was grown.

In common with many dales villages

High Mill at Westgate.

and towns, Westgate was once an important centre for cockfighting and the site of the old cock pit is still visible high on the fellside, above the village.

Westgate and Eastgate were once, literally, the gates to the Prince Bishops' hunting park, and Westgate was once the site of their quite substantial castle. It was a strong, crenellated building, bordered on two sides by the Middlehope Burn and the River Wear. It had a large main chamber plus smaller chambers for guests, out-houses, courtyards and stabling for the horses, although there are now only scant remains. In Queen Elizabeth's day the bishop's bailiffs met here to conduct forest business. If a farmer had died, his son, or widow, would be required to attend the Forest Court to be sworn in as the new tenant and for this privilege they paid a fee known as a 'Jack-penny'.

Westgate was also well-known for lead mining. Just a short walk along Middlehope Burn, is the Slit Shaft which, at 585ft, was one of the deepest in the North Pennines. The miners negotiated this by ladders. The valley floor here was so narrow and tight that the burn was covered to provide more working space. Nature is regaining a hold on the area, softening the

harsh industrial landscape, but the bousesteads, level mouths and bridge abutments are still visible as silent monuments to those Victorian miners who left a permanent scar on the valley.

Several mines operated in the area surrounding the village. It was a busy industrial centre, a huge contrast to the quiet residential and farming community that exists here today.

Wesley's Tree, Ireshopeburn

METHODISM with its simple, uncomplicated doctrine has always had a powerful influence on the farmers and miners of Weardale. It began in 1748 with a

The thorn tree where John Wesley preached at Ireshopeburn.

Burnhope Reservoir, with Burnhope Seat in the background.

visit to Westgate from the itinerant preacher Christopher Hopper, a Methodist schoolmaster from Newcastle. The movement grew and visits from other preachers followed in 1749.

John Wesley first came to the dale in 1752 and his visits continued periodically until 1790. Such was his following that his congregations were often very large, and to accommodate them he had to preach in the open. On one of these occasions, in 1774, he is believed to have preached under a hawthorn tree at Ireshopeburn. As a tribute to the man, and the event, this spot is marked today with a commemorative plaque.

West Blackdene

THE village of West Blackdene was probably one of the earliest settlements in Upper Weardale. Its origin dates back to the 13th-century clearance of the Weardale Forest for pastoral farming. It was these early beginnings that heralded the change of the hunting park character of the upper dale.

Cottages in the village of West Blackdene.

Cottages were added to the northern side in the early part of the 19th century to house workers from the nearby mine and the bridge was built in 1848 to connect the village with Ireshopeburn.

The village was originally built on the enclosure style with a central walled animal pound. This pound has been cultivated to a most attractive garden, enhancing and blending with the character of this charming upper dales village.

Burnhope Reservoir

BURNHOPE Reservoir is situated high on the fellside above the village of Wearhead. It was built as a result of just one of the campaigns of Peter Lee, the chairman of Britain's first Labour council which was elected here in County Durham. He was a great Labour leader and workers' champion and fought vigorously for a decent living for the common people.

The reservoir was begun

in 1930 and was opened in 1937, a fine monument to a tireless campaigner.

Sedling Mine

THE Sedling Lead Mine was situated in a quiet valley to the north of Cowshill in Upper Weardale. It was operated by the Beaumont Company from 1818 until 1878. During this period the mine produced over 10,000 tons of lead. The mineshaft was over 400ft deep and descended to a rich vein that was 8ft to 12ft thick.

After 1848 the mine was taken over by the Weardale Lead Company and they developed two new offshoots and the production, during their ownership, was over 17,000 tons of lead ore 'galena'.

Between 1900 and 1916 the operation produced nearly 50,000 tons of fluorspar and only about 3,000 tons of lead ore, consequently the mine became principally known for its fluorspar; this was mainly extracted at High Sedling from workings near the surface. Today, the deeply scarred hillsides serve as a stark indication of the huge yield.

The Sedling Mine was closed in 1948 when the last oreshoot was finally exhausted. However, in 1966 there was an attempt to extract fluorspar by opencast methods but the collapsing of old workings stopped this venture.

The valley is quiet today, the silence broken only by farmers going about their daily tasks and occasional walkers using the old lead roads on their way to Race Head and Rookhope, over the windswept fell.

Killhope Lead Mining Centre

KILLHOPE Lead Mining Centre is set high in the North Pennines Area of Outstanding Natural Beauty, almost at the head of Weardale. At an altitude of over 1,500ft it must be England's highest tourist attraction, and this is part of the fascination of the site. The story of 19th-century lead mining is re-created exactly where it happened, in the sometimes harsh, but always beautiful, upland scenery.

Richard Watson, the Teesdale poet and leadminer, described the North Pennines as '*these hollow hills*', illustrating the extent to which the fells had become honeycombed with shafts and tunnels by men in their search for lead. This was no understatement and at the beginning of the 19th century this area was the most productive lead ore field in the world.

The Park Level Mine at Killhope was opened in 1853 and 20 years later the crushing mill was built — until then all the crushing and dressing of the ore had been done by hand. At its peak the site was producing almost 2,500 tonnes of lead ore a year for the smelt mills and employed 110 men under-

Sedling Rake, Weardale.

Crushing mill and Killhope Wheel.

Bouseteams at Killhope Lead Mining Centre.

ground, assisted by 30 boys at the surface.

Unfortunately, in the late 1800s the price of lead halved to a low of £9 10s 0d per ton and the industry went into decline. Unable to face competition from cheaper, imported lead, Killhope closed just after the turn of the century, and the machinery and equipment were removed from the site. Nature reclaimed its hold, softening and mellowing this man-made scar on the landscape.

In 1970 Durham County Council acquired the derelict site with plans to tidy it up for use as a picnic area, but their investigations revealed an exciting find — the most complete remains of the Victorian lead mining industry in Britain. Killhope started a new life and under the expert guidance of site manager, Ian Forbes, was transformed into an exciting and dramatic step back into living history.

A visit to Killhope begins with a walk through the Visitor Centre exhibition which provides an introduction to the social aspect of the lead miners' lives. The exhibition draws heavily on the personal records of Joseph Graham, a miner who emigrated to America in the 1850s in search of a better life. He settled and prospered on a small farm in New York State but still kept in touch with the large family he left behind, They wrote often, keeping him up-to-date with news of Killhope and the dale.

These letters describe in vivid detail the difficulties and hardships endured by the miners and their families — their joys and sorrows and their lives and deaths. It was Joseph Graham's great-granddaughter who presented this material to Killhope and she travelled from the USA to be present at the official opening of the exhibition in May 1991.

Once through the exhibition, it is out on to the site. A visit to the mineshop reveals such facilities as stabling for the ponies, and the blacksmith's shop, which would also make and repair tools; here, too, was the mine office, centre of administration, where every transaction was carefully recorded. It was also in the mineshop that some miners lodged. These places were notorious for their overcrowded and dirty conditions — the men would often sleep four to a bed and they cooked their meals in a communal frying pan. Drying work clothes gave off clouds of harmful dust, the men developed lung diseases and many died in their early 40s.

The miners did not work directly for the company but were self-employed,

working in gangs of three to ten men. They struck a bargain to work part of the mine and were paid on output. Some became wealthy but many more lived hard and brief lives in poverty.

Rock, or 'bouse', was loaded into pony-drawn tubs, brought out of the mine and tipped into 'bouse teams' — each gang of men had its own. Nearby the rock was washed in running water, enabling the young boys on the 'washing floor' to pick out pieces of silvery 'galena'. Large pieces of rock were bro-

Family fun as children gain 'hands-on' experience.

Waste material was tipped separately.

Underground water wheel in Park Level Mine.

ken up for further 'dressing' — the process of separating the lead ore from the other minerals. This washing process was repeated many times in many forms to separate every piece of lead ore. Any ore that was not readily separable was dealt with by the 'crushing mill'. The mill at Killhope was powered by a huge overshot steel waterwheel almost 34ft in diameter, and the largest in the north of England.

Extensive repair and major restoration by specialist engineers enabled this huge wheel to work again and now the tradition is that the first visitor of the day pulls the lever which starts the wheel turning.

Further separation of the rock was carried out in the 'jigger house' and finally the rock was stored on the terraces or 'bingsteads' to await transportation to the smelt mills at either nearby Allenheads, just over the border in Northumberland, or at Rookhope, further down Weardale.

The reservoirs and water systems which, together, powered the Killhope Wheel, are situated above the site, further up the fellside and illustrate the high degree of engineering that was required to keep the crushing mill operative.

Twentieth-century forestation has been imaginatively used to conceal several re-creations of early lead mining procedures, in clearings, linked by a woodland walk. The first mines were shallow pits dug along the line of a vein. These 'bell-pits' had hand rollers or 'stows' mounted over them for winding up 'kibbles', or buckets of galena. Workings from these shafts could not extend very far and when one shaft had progressed as far as possible, another was sunk further along the vein until eventually a line of abandoned shafts marked its course.

Shafts became deeper and the stow was replaced by the 'whimsey' — up to four horses would walk in a circle winding the mine ropes around a large drum mounted on heavy timbers.

There is also evidence of 'hushing'

above the site. This method of mining used water to wash away the topsoil, revealing the veins of lead ore. These huge, deep, gouges serve as a silent reminder of the powerful effectiveness of this 18th-century method of mining.

Killhope also has another surprise. Visitors can see 'the hollow hills' for themselves by venturing into the depths of Park Level Mine, to follow in the footsteps of the men who drove their tunnels deep into the hillside over a century ago. The level at Killhope was first driven through shale. This softer rock made the job easier and cheaper initially.

The miners were then able to work the mineral deposits in the limestone. The tunnel is a masterly piece of engineering, the walls are over 2ft thick and they can flex and move with the ground and yet provide the immense strength needed to support the excavations, a fine tribute to the skill of the mine masons.

Once through the tunnel, visitors come out into a huge 60ft high underground chamber, complete with a scenario of Victorian lead mining and an 18ft working waterwheel.

This added bonus of being able to sample the underground lives of these miners of the North Pennines must surely establish this Killhope experience as one of the finest in Britain.

Killhope Lead Mining Centre, Weardale.

Edmundbyers

THE village of Edmundbyers had its beginning in Saxon times, but takes its name from Edmund, King of Northumbria, who fought the Vikings in the north of England in the 9th century. 'Edmundbiers' is recorded in the *Boldon Book*, Northumbria's own *Domesday Book*, in 1183 as being held

St Edmund's Church.

by Alan Bruntoft, as reward for his service in the bishop's forest.

It is hard to believe that this quiet little village in north-west Durham, on the shores of the Derwent Reservoir, was well-known for its witchcraft in the 17th century. One woman, Margaret Hooper, in 1641 is reputed to have been possessed by the Devil himself, although she was thankfully saved by prayer and divine intervention. The most famous witchcraft trial, however, was held at Newcastle Assizes on 3 April 1673. Ann Armstrong, and John and Ann Whitfield of Edmundbyers, together with several others from the surrounding area, were shown to have attended a witches' meeting in the village. They were accused of causing death to livestock by changing shape and bewitching the poor unfortunate animals.

In those days fear and superstition caused blame to be laid on lonely old ladies and eccentric recluses for any incident that was not easily explained. The hysterical outcry against witchcraft caused many innocent people to be burned at the stake, or drowned, after being subject to the harsh and primitive tests to determine their guilt or innocence — although there can have been

little comfort in death proving the person's innocence, in some cases.

St Edmund's Church, at the western end of the village, was founded about 1150. There is possibly Saxon stonework incorporated into the structure but most is Norman, although the building was extensively restored in the 19th century. The altar is a single slab of a type forbidden in the 16th century when it was removed. It was rediscovered in 1855 and restored to its original use.

One of the windows in the church is an 'eye' window said to ward off evil spirits. A headstone in the west wall of the graveyard is in memory of Elizabeth Lee who died in 1792 and was reputed to be the last witch to live in Edmundbyers.

The village of Edmundbyers.

The Old Roads of County Durham

THE pleasure of country walking as a hobby is a fairly new idea, although the footpaths used are often very old. Drovers' roads, packhorse routes, salters' ways and ancient footpaths form a network criss-crossing the fells and dales of western County Durham. These ways were formed as very direct routes linking ancient market centres, their lines were often marked by roadside crosses or guide stones known as 'Stoops'. Travelling along the valleys must have been fraught with difficulty and hardship because of the swamps, forests and wild animals. Most travellers would therefore choose the higher ground where possible, thus many elevated routes evolved. At some places in Durham these ancient roads cross the fell tops at an altitude of almost 2,000ft. A few of them have been metalled and are now adventurous roads for cars, but many more are still green ways or tracks.

The greater use of wheeled vehicles eventually meant a move to more lowland lines of transport and the older upland tracks were left to 'salters', 'broggers', 'badgers' and 'drovers'.

Salt was a vital commodity in the past and was traded from earliest times. It was carried from the coast by teams of up to ten pack-ponies, linked together, each carrying up to 100lbs. They would be under the control of a salt trader or 'salter', as he would be known.

Salt was so important that it gave its name to many places along the trading routes — for instance Salters' Gate, near Tunstall Reservoir was on the main route from South Shields. Often a saltway was called a 'whiteway' and this name can still be seen on some maps. Salt roads are quite dif-

Salt Road, Salters' Gate.

Green Trod, drovers' road, Teesdale.

ficult to separate from other routes, except in their early stages where they can be linked directly with the coastal salt pans — further inland the market roads usually served the salters' purpose.

'Broggers' also used the market roads to ply their trade. They were licensed by the Halifax Acts of the 16th century to deal in small parcels of wool collected directly from the remote dales and villages for carriage to the larger markets.

'Badgers' were peddlars licensed to carry corn from the markets to sell in small quantities in the countryside, and to deal in all kinds of small goods and produce. Places like Badger Gate, Badger Stile and Badger Stoop have taken their name from these wandering traders.

The 'badger' was the country packman, or 'chapman', either carrying his pack, or 'chap' on his back or, if he was fortunate, using a pony for his load. No doubt his visit to the outlying farms was a great event. He would go into the big farm kitchen and spread out his wares: lace, ribbons, sewing materials, perfumes, simple medicines and sometimes even spices and flavourings. However, the most valuable thing he carried was news and gossip, which would be liberally dispensed while taking the refreshments provided when business was over. His customers were not only the farmer's wife but quite often the nearer neighbours, servants and workers would be invited too; his visit was, in this respect, an important social event.

The 17th century was a period marked by an extreme change in land ownership in the North Pennine Dales of County Durham, this was largely due to the break-up of common field

Holwick Scar, Teesdale.

Drovers' road from Side Head to Race Head (left), Carriers' Way, Carriers' Hill (right).

holdings. The final effect on this upheaval was the creation of the field system we know today. Many of these 'new' fields in the Upper Dales were used for the rearing and keeping of dairy cattle — this eventually led to a reduction in the amount of beef cattle being bred and butchers had to look elsewhere.

The hills of Scotland were regarded as ideal for breeding beef cattle but were not considered the best for fatten-ing, and it was this situation that led to the idea of importing Scottish cattle to be fattened in the Pennine Hills and Dales before sending them south to the large cattle marts which had sprung up further down the country. Thus cattle were bought at the Great Fairs or 'Trysts' in Falkirk, Crieff or Dumfries by the 'graziers' or cattle dealers, who would then make their arrangements for driving the cattle south to the lush Pennine Dales. A dealer would often

have several drovers working for him on a regular basis and it was not uncommon for these men to bring cattle south to be offered for sale at local farms, and be entrusted to take back the price in cash to their employers.

The herds of cattle were brought south by ways which avoided the towns and cultivated areas, keeping, as far as possible, to the fells and open moors, crossing streams and rivers near to their source, or by well-established fords.

The 'drover' had, perhaps, a boy and two dogs for his company, and herded 40 or 50 beasts. Companies of drovers would sometimes bring 100-200 head of cattle, with a man for each 40 or 50 beasts and several mules to carry their possessions.

The progress along these routes was gentle. The cattle would feed occasionally on the way and were found a good resting place at night, after a day's trek of 10 or 12 miles. Usually a short halt would be called at mid-day to allow grazing, and in the evening a sheltered, grassy hollow, with water nearby, was found for the overnight stop. After long use these spots, or 'stances', would produce a crop of fine grass — they can still be recognised in places. Later, in the 18th century, small enclosures near lonely inns or farmhouses would be used, for a small fee. Several of these drovers inns, with their now broken enclosure walls, can still be seen. The repeated passage of hundreds of cattle by the same routes created green ways, sometimes 20 or 30 yards wide, on the open fells, and also cut deep, sunken ways on the crests of hills.

Probably one of the finest examples of a drovers' road in County Durham is

Stanhope Ford, an ancient crossing point on the River Wear.

'The Green Trod'. It enters the county from Cumbria in spectacular fashion, winding over the great whinstone outcrop of Cronkley Scar, and continuing along the high fells, edging the Upper Tees Valley, to the tiny hamlet of Holwick. From here it leads south to Lunedale and Baldersdale, across God's Bridge over the River Greta, and on to Sleightholme before entering into Arkengarthdale and North Yorkshire.

It was not only cattle that were moved along the drovers' roads. They were also used for moving sheep, pigs, and even geese to and from the markets.

God's Bridge, Pennine Way, Teesdale.

Long-distance droving began in the Middle Ages and continued right up until the advent of the railways. So the next time you are following the course of one of these comfortable country footpaths, spare a thought for the salters, broggers, badgers and drovers who passed this way before.

Western County Durham: Teesdale

Cockfield

WHERE else in the county is there a village of such multiple interest as Cockfield?

Iron Age settlements, Roman occupation, a 13th-century church, abandoned bell pit coal workings and waggonways would all make this an interesting location long before the Dixon brothers made their mark on Cockfield and the world.

The Vavasours, early lords of the manor, are recorded mining coal here in 1375. This is possibly the earliest documented inland coal mine, at a time when overland transporting of coal was so difficult and expensive. Not until the coming of the Stockton & Darlington Railway with its branch line over Cockfield Fell, would it be possible to sell coal further afield than the immediate area.

Cockfield Fell.

Jeremiah Dixon's House, Cockfield.

Cockfield Fell.

The Vavasours were buried in Cockfield's unpretentious church which belies its great antiquity, having a core of 13th-century origin. Disguised though it is, by subsequent extensions over the centuries, it contains many interesting features.

It was two brothers, descendants of George Dixon, the remarkable steward to the 2nd Lord Barnard, who brought fame to the village.

George Dixon (1731-85) was mainly a self-taught man, becoming a mathematician, engineer, chemist, geologist, engraver, painter and draughtsman. He pioneered in hydraulics and pneumatics but his great achievement came in 1760 when he invented coal gas lighting. The family home, Garden House, Cockfield, became the first to be lit by coal gas.

Jeremiah Dixon (1733-79) was also largely self-taught, although both

The unique Skew Bridge.

brothers received some tuition in mathematics. He became a government appointed astronomer and surveyor. In 1763 he was appointed with another surveyor, Charles Mason, of the Royal Society, to survey and determine the bitterly-disputed boundary between the American colonies of Pennsylvania and Maryland, a considerable task, partly through virgin forest and Indian territories. This was achieved by 1767 and is to this day known as 'the Mason-Dixon Line'.

Upon his return he developed his plans for a canal system in the Cockfield area but these never came to fruition, so saving Cockfield from excessive industrialisation, just as Durham City's canalisation plans, if effected, would have changed a beautiful city into an inland port.

The Skew Bridge, The Gaunless Valley

A SHORT walk from the disused Haggerleases Quarry, near Butterknowle, along the abandoned flat trackbed of the railway, leads to a remarkable feat of civil engineering: the Skew Bridge, so named because it crosses the river at the very acute angle of 27 degrees. To construct a bridge to this specification in 1830 was quite a challenge, and the railway company had to go all the way to the North Riding of Yorkshire, to James Wilson of Pontefract, who built them one to last and is remembered by the plaque on the north side of the bridge.

A local name for the bridge was the 'Swin Bridge' — 'swin' being skew or 'at an angle' in dialect. When the Ordnance Surveyor came to the area in the 1850s he mistook the name and wrote on the first edition of the Ordnance Survey Map, 'The Swing Bridge'.

At one time this was a bustling industrial site with steam locomotives hauling and shunting coal trucks beside a rather dirty river and it had been so since 1830 when the Stockton & Darlington Railway opened its Haggerleases branch line until 1963 when British Rail closed it down.

Today it is a very peaceful rural scene — the only sounds are from the cool, clear water of the River Gaunless with the occasional heron waiting in the still pools, the blue flash of the kingfisher going about its daily business, and the busy dipper feeding in the clean water.

Copley Smelt Mill Chimney

COPLEY Smelt Mill operated from 1790 to 1890 and was supplied with coal from local collieries. It was unique in that it was located away from the lead ore fields of Teesdale. Nothing much remains of the smelt mill except the manager's house on the north side of the site and the 115ft-high chimney to the south. This tapered, round, sandstone chimney stands at the end of a long flue, long since collapsed and filled in, but which at one time zig-zagged its way up the hillside. The chimney would carry the toxic fumes from the smelter and belch them out high above the valley into the Gaunless air.

The mill was owned and operated by

(left) Copley chimney and (right) Steele Road near Butterknowle.

the Lords of Raby who were entitled to a tithe of all ore mined on their estate. The nearest lead mines were on Egglestone Common and near Middleton-in-Teesdale, but because it was more economical, the lead ore — galena — was transported by ponies to the Copley Smelt Mill; on the return journey they would carry coal for the Egglestone Smelt Mills.

Lead smelts easily, but since galena is a sulphide it gives off sulphurous gases which have to be dispersed because they could do serious harm to the smelters — hence the flues and the chimney, although the chimney would also serve to increase the flow of air through the smelting furnace. The present chimney dates from 1832 and may well have been a new addition to the mill at that time or, possibly, a rebuild of the original.

Lead was brought to the mill along the Steel, or Steele, Road, which runs westward from the site; it is a public footpath and can be followed all the way to Egglestone via Woolly Hill; the pack ponies with their panniers of galena had a rough passage and consequently some of the silvery galena was spilled on to the road, giving it a sheen like burnished steel — hence the name.

Hamsterley, 'The Castles'

AT THE edge of Hamsterley Forest, on private farmland, is a large and remark-

'The Castles', possibly an Ancient British camp.

able construction. It is believed, by some historians, to be an Ancient British camp, and is marked on the Ordnance Survey Map as 'The Castles'.

This is a very interesting and unusual site with tumbled stonework in a glade on the side of a south-facing slope. The whole camp is surrounded by a deep gully on three sides and a small stream, which has cut a deep V-shaped valley, on the fourth. The site is enclosed by four walls of substantial

Raby Castle.

stonework, in some places over 10ft wide, and there is enough material to suggest a height of over 10ft, too. On the eastern side is an entrance, the main one to the enclosure. This was reconstructed by an amateur archaeologist and purports to show a small guard chamber beside the doorway. No artifacts have been found on the site, no pot shards, weapons or relics. However, in one corner, the arm bones of a young woman were discovered. Did she live here or was she the victim of some dastardly crime in this most inaccessible of places?

This is certainly an enigmatic and atmospheric site which provides much material for speculation as to its origin and purpose.

Raby Castle

RABY CASTLE is one of County Durham's most impressive fortresses. It is set in a beautiful landscaped park where flocks of sheep, a herd of longhorn cattle and, of course, the famous Raby herds of red and fallow deer freely roam.

The castle is the family seat of the Lord Barnard whose extensive estates reach as far south as Cumbria to the west, and Yorkshire to the south.

The origins of the castle go back to the time of King Cnut in the 9th century, although it was only a relatively crude fort in those days. In the 12th century the estate came into the possession of the Neville family. It was

Geoffrey Neville, son of Isabella de Neville, an influential Norman heiress, who became the first Lord of Raby. A succession of Nevilles followed and the family became even more powerful. The size of the family home increased in proportion and eventually, in the 14th century, a licence to crenellate was granted by Thomas Hatfield, Prince Bishop of Durham. At this time the Lord of Raby was John Neville, the son of Ralph who was hero of the Battle of Nevilles Cross, fought on the outskirts of Durham City in 1346.

The Nevilles held Raby until the 16th century. In 1569 the 'Rising of the North' — a plan to replace Elizabeth I with Mary, Queen of Scots — was plotted at Raby. It was a catastrophic failure and the estate was seized by the Crown.

Sir Henry Vane, Secretary of State to Charles I, purchased Raby in 1626. During the Civil War, the Vanes fought on the side of Parliament and this resulted in the only time the castle was ever stormed, by a Royalist force. Sir Henry's son, of the same name, was beheaded after the restoration of Charles II.

The Vanes regained Raby during the reign of William II and it was he who bestowed on them the title, 'The Lords Barnard'.

True to the tradition of many English castles, Raby is reputed to be haunted, not by the Nevilles, as one would imagine, but by a former Lady Barnard, known as 'Old Hell Cat', who it is said, can be seen on the ramparts at dusk, knitting furiously with red-hot needles.

The walled garden, set a little way from the castle, is beautifully designed and maintained. It is a timeless, peaceful place — a spot to quietly sit and reflect upon the wonderful history of this magnificent family and their estate.

The picturesque Raby Castle gardens.

Winston Bridge

THE manor of Winston dates from earliest times and originally belonged to the powerful Nevilles, but in 1313 it was granted to the Scropes of Masham. The village still retains its quiet charm and overlooks the Tees from a height of nearly 200ft — a position which affords excellent views across the valley. The valley is spanned by what is possibly one of the finest examples of an old coaching bridge in England.

The old coaching bridge at Winston.

Winston Bridge was built by Sir Thomas Robinson of Rokeby in 1764 and has a single span of 111ft. At the time of its construction it was considered to be the largest bridge of a single span in Europe. It does, however, enjoy the distinction of being one of the few bridges over the Tees not to have been washed away in the Great Flood of 1771.

The Castle, Barnard Castle

BARNARD CASTLE stands proudly on an 80ft rocky river cliff above the sparkling River Tees. The first fortification on the site is thought to have been a small earthwork with a palisade which was constructed by Guy de Baliol, who had been granted the surrounding lands for his faithful service to William the Conqueror. Its original purpose would have been to protect the point where the old Roman road forded the river. Guy was succeeded by his nephew, Bernard, and his son, also named Bernard. It was these two men who were mainly responsible for the development of the site. They transformed the earthworks into a huge stone castle and it is from these two men that it takes its name, Bernard's Castle, or as it has become known, Barnard Castle.

Barnard Castle overlooking the River Tees.

Some of the later Baliols were of a different nature and Sir Hugh Baliol, in the time of King John, indulged excessively in his passion for plundering and personal gain. It would seem that this lawless behaviour did him no harm because King John himself was a guest at the castle in 1216. This trait was obviously not passed down to his son, John, because he was the founder of the celebrated Baliol College, Oxford. He was married to Devorguilla, the daughter of the Lord of Galloway, and as such became Regent of Scotland. After his death his wife built Sweetheart Abbey, near Dumfries, in his memory.

She kept his embalmed heart with her, in an ivory casket, for the rest of her life and when she died, it was buried alongside her in the abbey, a touching love story. Their youngest son, also called John, was chosen from 13 claimants by Edward I to be the rightful heir to the Scottish throne. He was crowned king at Scone after swearing allegiance to the English king. However, four years later he changed his mind and rebelled. He was defeated, his lands confiscated and he was incarcerated in the Tower of London. Thus the Baliols occupation of Barnard Castle ended.

The Bishops of Durham had always laid claim to Barnard Castle and the downfall of the Baliols presented Bishop Anthony Bek with the wonderful opportunity to take up residence. He added to the existing building and is credited with the rebuilding of the massive keep. The bishop remained in possession of the castle for five years but was eventually obliged to pass it back to the Crown. The castle, along with the Barony of Gainford, was then

granted to the Beauchamps, the Earls of Warwick, and remained in their possession for five generations. At the death of Richard Neville, famous as 'Warwick the Kingmaker' during the Wars of The Roses, the castle was passed to his daughter, Anne. Thus it passed to her husband, and they lived there until he was crowned King Richard III in 1483. He was killed at Bosworth Field and the castle passed to his enemy, the victor of the battle, Henry VII.

The new religion introduced by Henry VIII still caused disquiet in the north, even into the early years of the reign of Elizabeth I because she, too, gave it her firm support. This led to the 'Rising of the North', planned by the Percys, Earls of Northumberland and the Nevilles, Earls of Westmorland. Their intention was to restore the old religion and release Mary, Queen of Scots, from captivity in Bolton Castle in Wensleydale, and place her on the English throne. It was during this rebellion that the castle came under heavy siege. Sir George Bowes, steward to Queen Elizabeth, held out for ten days against 5,000 rebels with artillery. Eventually, treachery, desertion and the cutting-off of his water supply forced him to surrender, although he was allowed to march out of the castle with 400 of his men. This delay had been most helpful and allowed the Earl of Sussex to gather an army and finally crush the rebellion. As a mark of gratitude for his sterling service the castle was granted to Sir George Bowes and remained with his family until 1603. It was then given by James I to his infamous favourite, Robert Carr, Earl of Somerset. When Carr fell from grace in 1615, because of his involvement in the death by poison-

ing of Sir Thomas Overbury, the castle passed to the estate of the Prince of Wales.

It was eventually sold to Sir Henry Vane, Secretary of State to Charles I. Sir Henry ordered the castle to be dismantled to provide materials for the repair and extensive rebuilding of his main residence, Raby Castle. Thus the use of Barnard Castle as a fortress came to a sad end. In 1952 the Lord Barnard of Raby placed the castle in the care of what is now English Heritage, allowing everyone the opportunity to visit this romantic ruin in its dramatic setting.

Barnard Castle Bridge

LINKING County Durham with what was North Yorkshire, the bridge at Barnard Castle is overshadowed by its impressive neighbour, the castle itself. No less interesting, however, the bridge has an unusual history and is linked with many fascinating stories.

The earliest record of a bridge at Barnard Castle is 1327 but this was probably not the one we see today. We hear of a bridge mentioned again in 1422 when it was said that Catterick Bridge was reputed to be a copy of that at Barnard Castle. The existing bridge could possibly date from the 13th or 14th centuries, although the 13th century does, perhaps, seem the more likely because there was a huge increase in bridge building at that time to replace existing fords. In his *History of Durham,* Surtees says that the bridge was repaired in 1569 after being damaged during the Rising of the North.

In the 18th century the bridge had a chapel at its centre where illegal marriages were conducted by a man named

Barnard Castle Bridge spanning the River Tees.

Cuthbert, son of a clergyman from Denton called Alexander Hilton. Cuthbert had taken no holy orders — in fact the nearest he came to religious qualifications was that he had been trained as a Bible clerk by his father. He performed the services with enthusiasm, between two counties. This was a clever move because neither group of authorities felt they had the power to remove him.

The bridge was seriously damaged in the Great Flood of 1771 and had to be rebuilt afterwards. The arch on the south side could not cope with the vast increase in the flow of water and the retaining wall collapsed under the awesome power. The water gushed into the street, washing everything away down to the bare rock, leaving a 12ft difference in height between the bridge and the road. Horses were unable to cross and the only access for pedestrians was by ladder.

There is also the amusing tale of a dyer who was putting his cloth through its last stages of the process when the flood occured. He abandoned his material in the 'kettles', or rock pools, where he had been working. After the waters subsided he returned and after cleaning the mud and silt from his cloth, saw to his great surprise that it had been dyed far better than ever before. This new cloth sold so well that there was a huge demand for more — unfortunate and frustrating for the dyer, of course, because he could not supply.

The bridge, with its two fine pointed arches, is regarded as a good example of the Gothic Style and, hopefully, will continue to carry traffic across the Tees for many years to come.

The Market Cross, Barnard Castle

BARNARD CASTLE is a particularly attractive market town with a most

unusual market cross. It was built in 1747 at the expense of its worthy and generous citizen, Thomas Breaks, and it stands defiantly astride the A688 at the southern end of the Market Place, seeming to challenge approaching traffic which has to negotiate around it. Surely this is County Durham's most unusual traffic island.

In its time it has been town hall, courthouse, lock-up, fire station and butter market. It is capped with a cupola-style belfry finished with a gilded weather-vane. Rarely has a relatively small ground space been put to such extended use and been incorporated within such an architectural gem. In the town it is, however, simply and confusingly referred to as 'The Market Cross'.

The weather-vane's two puncture holes are attributed to conflicting explanations, but the most authentic would seem to be that they result from a competition between a Barnard Castle rifleman and one of the Earl of Strathmore's gamekeepers in 1804 when they fired at this target from over a 100 yards distance, along the Market Place from the Turk's Head inn.

Today the local people are much safer company. Residents and visitors mingle happily, enjoying the numerous attractions and facilities for which Barnard Castle has gained such a reputation.

The John and Josephine Bowes Museum

THE John and Josephine Bowes Museum is probably one of the biggest surprises in Teesdale, an enormous build-

(opposite) The splendid Market Cross, Barnard Castle.

The John and Josephine Bowes Museum at Barnard Castle.

ing constructed in the sumptuous Renaissance style of a French chateau. It was founded in the second half of the 19th century by John Bowes, the illegitimate son of the 10th Earl of Strathmore, and his French wife, Josephine. John Bowes was born in 1811 and, although he inherited his father's estates, he was not recognised as heir to the Strathmore title.

The Bowes family first arrived in Teesdale at the time of the Norman Conquest and eventually gained vast estates in Durham and Yorkshire. Their lands were rich in coal and they accumulated great wealth through its mining and transportation. From 1847, John Bowes spent a lot of his time in France. He owned a theatre in Paris and it was here that he met Josephine Benoite, the actress who was to become his wife.

They shared a great love of the arts and, indeed, Josephine herself was a talented painter. They married in 1852 and moved into the 17th-century Chateau du Barry, near Paris, a wedding present from John to his new wife. The house had been badly damaged during the Revolution and they set about its redecoration and furnishing in the latest French style.

Their passion for collecting continued to flourish and they decided, at Josephine's suggestion, to sell their house in Paris and buy land at Barnard Castle on which to build a museum specially for the purpose of housing their ever-expanding collection.

The museum was designed by two architects combining their talents, Jules Pellechet, a Frenchman and John Edward Watson, an Englishman. Josephine Bowes laid the foundation stone on 27 November 1869. Sadly, John and Josephine died — Josephine at the early age of 44, in 1875, and John in 1885 — before their museum was opened to the public on 10 June 1892. At first the museum was in the care of a

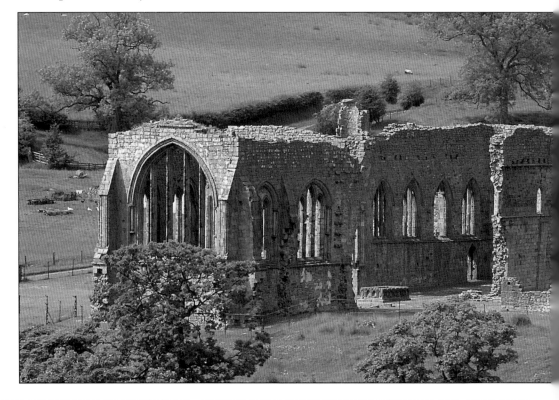

group of trustees but they ran into frequent financial problems. The trusteeship was transferred to Durham County Council in 1956, not only preventing the closure of the museum, but giving it a new lease of life. The collection has grown considerably since the time of John and Josephine and the museum is regarded as one of the finest treasure houses in Europe. It contains many fine examples of porcelain, paintings, tapestries, furniture, clothes, glass, gold and silver.

The most famous and, perhaps, the best-loved piece is the automated life-size musical Silver Swan in the entrance hall. It is thought to date from 1773. It was bought by John and Josephine from a Parisian jeweller in 1872 at a cost of 5,000 francs, or £200.

The Swan is controlled by three separate clockwork motors, these were built by the inventor, John Joseph Merlin. When it is set in motion it appears to preen itself and then majestically

bends its neck to take a fish from the water.

The John and Josephine Bowes Museum also has a royal connection. Her Majesty Queen Elizabeth the Queen Mother is descended from the 11th Earl of Strathmore. John Bowes' uncle, whose father married Mary Eleanor Bowes, the last in the family line, was obliged to take her name in order to gain the family inheritance, and thus a link was forged between the Bowes and the Royal Family.

Egglestone Abbey

THE nearest date that can be ascertained for the foundation of Egglestone Abbey is 1198, by Ralph de Multon for the White Canons of the Premonstratensian Order, who also gave Blanchland, on the Northumberland border, its name. The order was first founded in Premontre in northern France in 1121 by St Norbert, a wandering

Egglestone Abbey enjoys a tranquil setting on the wooded banks of the River Tees.

Bow Bridge, Thorgill Beck.

preacher from Germany. The first English monastery of the order was founded in 1143 — all together there were 33 houses of the Premonstratensian Order in England and Wales, two of them for women. These canons wore white habits to distinguish them from the Augustinian Order who wore black.

The abbey enjoys a tranquil setting on the wooded banks of the River Tees. Life for the monks was not as peaceful as the setting would suggest. They had a difficult time, constantly being the subject of border raids by the armies of both sides and although it enjoyed the status of an abbey, Egglestone always suffered poverty. When the Scots raided Yorkshire in 1315, the canons' losses were so great that their assessment for taxation was halved. In 1328 they were pardoned by Edward III for arrears of taxes amounting to £16 2s 7d, outstanding from the reign of his father. Things were so bad in 1332 that Archbishop Melton granted them a loan of £20.

The canons suffered heavy losses again when the northern barons enjoyed their 'hospitality' while raising an army before marching to beat the Scots at the Battle of Nevilles Cross in 1346. Even with the Scots out of the way, the position did not improve for the canons and they continued to be relieved from payment of taxes to the King and in the writ for the levy of a tithe (tenth) of their goods they were given exemption '*on account of their notorious poverty*'.

Usually there were 15 canons at the abbey but the constant financial pressure must have taken its toll because the level of religious commitment was not high and in 1502 it is recorded that there were serious offences against discipline. The last Abbot of Egglestone made a final surrender of its house and possessions to the King's representative in 1540.

After the Dissolution the site was granted to Robert Strelly and it was he who converted part of the buildings into a private dwelling. The property eventually passed to his nephews, the sons of his brother-in-law, George Savile.

In 1770 Sir Thomas Robinson sold the property to John Morritt of Rokeby, the well-known traveller and classical scholar. It descended through the generations of the Morritt family and in 1925, Major Henry Edward Morritt placed the ruins into the care of what is now English Heritage.

Just to the north of the abbey is Thorgill Beck which is crossed by Bow Bridge, a narrow 17th-century packhorse bridge with characteristic low parapets to allow the passage of the animals carrying large loads. This little bridge, sadly no longer in use, is a charming treasure, almost hidden from view in the environs of the abbey.

Rokeby House

DURING the reign of Edward II, border unrest was rife in the north and the Rokeby family home was burned by the Scots in a raid following the Battle of

Bannockburn. The building was restored, but when the estate was bought in 1601 by William Robinson, a London merchant, he completely rebuilt the house. It was between 1725 and 1730 that Sir Thomas Robinson, who was destined to become one of the most distinguished amateur architects in Britain, built the present house in the beautifully proportioned Palladian style which was more usually associated with Northern Italy rather than Teesdale. From 1731 he added to and generally improved his creation and eventually finished with a house that was much more elaborate than he had originally planned. Heavy business and social commitments in London increasingly kept Sir Thomas away from his estate and eventually in 1769, he sold it, along with most of its contents, to John Sawrey Morritt. During his occupancy much was done to

improve the estate — the church, Abbey Bridge and Greta Bridge, which was to feature in the famous painting, were all built within ten years of each other. In 1791 the house passed to his son, John Bacon Sawrey Morritt, who owned it up to his death in 1843. He served as MP on two occasions, for Beverley from 1799-1802 and for Shaftesbury from 1818-20.

In his 50 years of ownership, J.B.S.Morritt added much to the artistic collection in the house, including the famous *Rokeby Venus*, bought in 1813. He was a great friend of Sir Walter Scott, and the writer dedicated his epic work *Rokeby* to him, which was written during frequent stays on the estate.

In 1843 Rokeby was inherited by J.B.S.Morritt's younger brother, William John Sawrey Morritt, who was MP for the North Riding of Yorkshire. A flamboyant character, he was well-

Rokeby House, Teesdale.

known for his yellow coach, drawn by four magnificent horses. At his death in 1874, the house went to his younger brother, Robert Ambrose. His occupancy coincided with the excitement of the Industrial Revolution and it was he who installed gas lighting in the house. He was also the first occupant for many years who had a large family — seven children — and made many alterations to the interior, although he made no radical changes to the exterior. Robert Ambrose Morritt died in 1890 and unfortunately his eldest son, Robert Alexander, was killed in the South African War in 1901, so the house passed to his second son, Henry Edward, and his American wife, Grace. The owners kindly allowed the house to be used as a convalescent home for

The graceful arch of Greta Bridge.

wounded servicemen during both world wars. Today it is open to the public, so everyone can share the pleasure of the wonderful house that this remarkable family have established in beautiful Teesdale.

Greta Bridge

THE elegant Greta Bridge was built in 1773 by John Sawrey Morritt, Lord of Rokeby, at a cost of £850.

In 1805 the bridge was immortalised in the watercolour painting by John Sell Cotman. He stayed on the Rokeby Estate at the invitation of John Bacon Sawrey Morritt, the second Morritt owner of Rokeby, for three weeks, to give Lady Rokeby painting lessons.

Charles Dickens and his illustrator,

Hablot K.Browne, stayed at the old coaching inn beside the bridge on their first night when they visited Teesdale in February 1838, while researching Dickens novel *Nicholas Nickleby*. Indeed Greta Bridge gets a special mention in the book:

> '…*The day dragged on uncomfortably enough, and about six o'clock that night he [Nicholas Nickleby] and Mr Squeers, and the little boys, and their united luggage were all put down together at the George and New Inn, Greta Bridge*'.

Bowes, St Giles' Church

THE Roman Fort, Lavatrae, which originally stood on the site on which the village of Bowes is built, was plundered for material for the construction of St Giles' Church. It has traces of Norman architecture still visible, although

St Giles' Church, Bowes.

The grave of William Shaw, who was the inspiration for the cruel 'Wackford Squeers'.

The 10th-century Bowes Castle.

the exterior was extensively restored in 1865. However, the interesting interior is largely late medieval.

The village also has a proud literary connection. Charles Dickens was a visitor in 1838 while carrying out research on the Yorkshire Boarding Schools for his book *Nicholas Nickleby*. It was here that he came across the grim 'William Shaw's Academy', and it was on this establishment that he based his fictional school 'Dotheboys Hall'.

William Shaw, upon whom the cruel bully 'Wackford Squeers' was based, is buried in St Giles' Churchyard, whilst inside the church is a memorial to a 19th-century villager, George Ashton Taylor, who died in 1822 at only 19 years of age. He is believed to have been one of the many tragic victims of Shaw's Academy. This moved Dickens so much that he used George Ashton Taylor as the model for the unfortunate 'Smike' in his novel.

John, who is said to have visited the castle on several occasions.

These dramatic ruins are now in the care of English Heritage.

Bowes Castle

THE imposing monument of Bowes Castle was built in 1170 for Henry II, on the site of the Roman fort of Lavatrae. Indeed, some Roman masonry was incorporated into its fabric. Although the massive construction dominates the site, the ramparts of the Roman fort can still be traced on the hillside above the River Greta.

The castle is, essentially, a large, moated keep of three storeys with walls 50ft high and 12ft thick. There have been no outer defensive walls and this would suggest its function was a watch tower or garrisoned outpost to guard the approach to Stainmore Pass. Its most distinguished visitor was King

The Butterstone, near Cotherstone

IN ANCIENT times England suffered repeated visitations of the plague. Many millions died of the dreaded, highly infectious disease. Even remote and beautiful areas such as Teesdale did not escape its ravages and beside the

The Butterstone, near Cotherstone.

moorland road between Cotherstone and Bowes, near to where the footpath from Baldersdale emerges, stands a most interesting survival of these dark times — the Butterstone. In order to contain the fast-spreading scourge by isolating the affected villages, outside provisions were delivered to such convenient points, chosen at a safe distance. In exchange, the grateful villagers left payment in the form of coins immersed in jars of limewater or vinegar, primitive types of disinfectant. Thus, trade to and from the village was able to continue, despite the pestilence.

Stones such as these were known as Butterstones or Bacon Stones and have survived the centuries to be referred to, nowadays, as Plague Stones.

Romaldkirk

ROMALDKIRK is one of the prettiest villages in Teesdale and looks much the same today as it did in the Middle Ages when the picturesque stone cottages were built around the three village greens.

The village pump can still be seen and was in constant use until 1936. The double stocks are not used now, but have been preserved for posterity, a reflection, perhaps, on the good living of the present-day villagers?

Another historic feature in the village is the pound, four walls forming a small enclosure into which the pounder, or pinder, would put straying animals. He was empowered to levy a fine of one penny for a horse and a halfpenny for cattle or sheep.

The village was mentioned in *Domesday Book* and it takes its name from a 10th-century Saxon church which was dedicated to the little-known St Romauld, who spent his life setting up groups of hermit monks in Italy.

The Saxon church was probably first sacked by marauding Norsemen but the land was also laid waste by Malcolm and his Scottish army in 1070. The building of the present church was begun in 1150, added to in 1280, with further extensive additions in 1360. St Romauld's Church is often referred to as the 'Cathedral of the Dales', a title that befits its excellent setting.

Kirkcarrion

HIGH on the fells where Teesdale and Lunedale meet there is a prominent

The village stocks, Romaldkirk.

St Romauld's and the village pump, Romaldkirk (left) and Kirkcarrion (right).

A storm gathering over Kirkcarrion.

and romantic landmark. A group of old Scots pines marks the site of an ancient tumulus or burial mound. It was excavated in 1804 and a cinerary urn and the bones of a Celtic prince were found. His name was Caryn and it is from him that the spot takes its name — Kirkcarrion, or Caryn's Castle.

A local legend tells of a curse on the tomb. It is said that when the moon is full, casting its eerie silver light on to the dark trees and the prehistoric mound, Caryn's ghost can be seen, stalking the surrounding fells, seeking revenge for the desecration and plundering of his ancient tomb.

Bronze Age Burial Mound, Egglestone

UNFORTUNATELY, many Bronze Age round barrows, as these constructions are called, have been destroyed over the years by cultivation, mining, quarrying,

Burial mound at Egglestone.

or building. However, several can still be seen in County Durham and Bell Sike, Hempstone Knoll, near the village of Egglestone, in Teesdale, is a fine example.

The round barrow is a very distinctive type of burial. The body was placed in a 'cist' — this was a construction of flat stone slabs arranged to form a coffin-like stone box — and then covered with a huge mound of earth. A round barrow would probably contain one or more of these cists. Archaeologists have calculated, from finds within, that these barrows were in use by Bronze Age and Neolithic folk over a long period of time, possibly in excess of 1,300 years.

County Bridge, Middleton-in-Teesdale

THE road heading south out of Middleton-in-Teesdale crosses the County Bridge. County Bridges are so named because the County Council are directly responsible for their care and maintenance. This bridge once linked County Durham with North Yorkshire, before the county boundaries were redrawn in 1974, effectively moving County Durham further south.

This graceful, single-arch bridge was built in 1811, spanning an ancient crossing point on the River Tees, a location chosen, no doubt, because of its proximity to the confluence of Hudeshope Beck and the Tees — the places where rivers met were considered magical by ancient people. They may well have been right. This is still a magical spot, just right to while away an hour or two, sitting on the river bank by the bridge in the company of the charming Tees.

St Mary's Church, Middleton-in-Teesdale

ST MARY'S Church in Middleton-in-Teesdale is unique. It has the only detached bell tower in County Durham. This was bequeathed by the Revd William Bell who was rector of the parish from 1549 to 1559. It is a two-storey, ivy-clad building with a pitched roof and mullioned windows constructed as part of the wall in the north-west corner of the churchyard. The belfry itself is reached by a newell staircase in the north-east corner of the building. Of the three bells in the tower only one is original, the other two being replaced in 1697 and 1790. The oldest, however, bears the fascinating inscription:

Crossing the River Tees, the County Bridge, Middleton-in-Teesdale.

'Tell soull knell at his ending and for his soull say one paternoster and one ave. ano.dni.1557.'

The present church was completed in 1886 and is a fine example of the Late Decorated style. It replaces the earlier St Mary's which was demolished in 1878, although the east window from this church can still be seen displayed in the churchyard. This window has two trefoil lights beneath a round arch and serves to demonstrate the Early Decorated style used in conjunction with the original Norman church built in 1170.

Despite the obvious disadvantages of being a bell-ringer at St Mary's during inclement weather, the fact that the belfry is unique in the county must more than compensate for any discomfort.

Coldberry Lead Mines

THE abandoned mineshop at Coldberry is regarded as the finest example in Teesdale and was listed by the Department of the Environment in 1988. The adjoining stables contain the original stalls and even the names of the last resident ponies are chalked on the walls, still faintly legible.

There is little evidence to suggest when workings first began at Coldberry. The first documented mention is in Lord Barnard's review of 10 September 1730, where it states that a lease to work the south-east area of the site was granted to a John Buxton for 21 years for the usual tithe of ore mined. Ten years later this lease was cancelled and a new one was granted to the Reverend Edmund Maynott. In the same year, 1740, a lease was granted to John Tidy for the Coldberry Low Vein, to the south-east of the present Coldberry Gutter. At this time the vein was worked by hushing, eventually creating one of the largest opencast workings in the north. Although there is no record of when work on the gutter first began, it does seem to have been worked for over 250 years, possibly even longer, to

(opposite) St Mary's Church, with detached belfry, Middleton-in-Teesdale.

The mineshop at Coldberry.

Interior of Newbiggin Chapel.

was drawn up on 30 August 1759. Three itinerant preachers who spent much time in the area signed the indenture: Christopher Hopper, Matthew Lowes and Jacob Rowell, along with four local lead miners — Thomas Allinson of Bowlees, John Ridley and James Ainsley of Woodside and John Spence of Sievy Lee. They bought a small piece of land 20 yards long and 14 yards wide on which to build the meeting house. In his diary Jacob Rowell left an account of the expenses incurred in the building of the chapel: the total cost was £61 13s 5d. The erection of the roof came to £2 14s 0d and the roofing timbers cost £9 11s 1d. When completed the building would seat 200.

The chapel had a Sunday School in operation by 1830 and hymn books and copies of *Pilgrim's Progress* were offered as prizes. If pupils gained a high enough standard of merit they would be presented with a Bible on leaving. The London Lead Company was the major employer in the area and a great supporter of the Sunday School and its work. They gave London Lead Company Bibles to scholars who passed a Religious Education examination and they also bought books for the school library.

Several alterations were made to the building at its centenary. A new south wall was built, its height was raised and the roof was replaced. In 1880 a scheme was organised to construct a purpose-built Sunday School with cottages or flats above. However, these were to be sold off over 100 years later to finance restoration work.

Today the inside of the chapel still

retains its original features, complete with the old black stove and tiered seating. Many interesting old photographs, books, documents and artefacts are on display, providing an interesting insight into the history of the chapel and the village, and, as a reminder of John Wesley, who preached here.

Wynch Bridge

WYNCH BRIDGE crosses the River Tees just below Low Force Waterfall. It is

The exciting and unusual Wynch Bridge, surviving since 1830.

Gibson's Cave and Summerhill Force.

an unusual but picturesque sight, a footbridge out of the ordinary. This is the second bridge to occupy this site. The original was built in 1704 and was claimed to be the first suspension bridge in England, if not, Europe. It was built to allow leadminers to cross the river from their homes in Holwick, which was then in Yorkshire, to the mines high on the fells above Newbiggin.

The first bridge was a precarious affair — it was only one plank wide and only had one handrail! The experience of crossing this early bridge is dramatically described by the Durham historian, Hutchinson: *'It is planked in such a manner that the traveller experiences all the tremulous motion of the chains and sees himself suspended over a roaring gulf on an agitated restless gangway to which few strangers dare trust themselves.'*

Predictably, perhaps, the first bridge collapsed in 1820 while a party of nine haymakers were crossing; one man was killed when he was thrown into the narrow, rocky gorge below.

The present bridge dates from 1830, and, although it is not as terrifying to cross as that described by Hutchinson, it still provides an exciting and unusual way to cross the foaming Tees.

Gibson's Cave

THE Nature Trail from Bowlees Picnic Area in Upper Teesdale leads eventually to an attractive waterfall known as Summerhill Force, where the Bowlees Beck tumbles over the dark, slowly weathering limestone. Over the centuries the underlying softer shale beds and sandstone have been eroded by the action of the water, creating a dark, deep cave, hidden behind the waterfall.

This is a secluded and romantic spot. Local tradition tells of a 16th-century local outlaw named William Gibson who retreated here whenever he was being hunted by the constables of Barnard Castle. He was reputed to be a 'lovable rogue' and his family, and local people, would supply him with food and dry clothing while he sheltered in the safety of his dark, secret hideaway. When the hue and cry had passed he would come out of hiding to resume his cavalier lifestyle until his nefarious activities forced his return to the secret place nature had so kindly provided behind the silvery screen.

This is indeed a place to linger awhile, for there is much to appreciate from Mother Nature, and, rest assured, the constables of Barnard Castle are busy elsewhere!

Carr Crags

STRETCHING for about half a mile along the 2,000ft contour, high above the Flushiemere Beck in Upper Teesdale, is an outcrop of millstone grit known as Carr Crags. This area has been extensively worked for gateposts, troughs, and most impressively, millstones. There are over 20 of these to be found, scattered at random, in various stages of completion, along the outcrop. Some seem as if they were just laid there yesterday and others lie half buried by the insidious creeping of the peat.

Locals say production ceased early in the 20th century, but no one seems to know for certain when it began — some suggest the early 19th century while others believe the area may well have been worked much earlier.

The real curiosity of the site is undoubtedly the group of cup-marked boulders found towards the northern extremity of the outcrop — none of these strange markings are to be found anywhere else on the site. The decoration would appear to be on the natural bed of the rocks and only one boulder shows these cups on a vertical face, but this one may well have been upturned. These deep marks do not seem to have been made by any reasonably recent industrial process and some historians do believe them to be prehistoric. If they are prehistoric then this would perhaps lend some credence to the theory that a stone circle exists dispersed within this disturbance of boulders.

Certainly, an unnatural arrangement of huge rocks is to be observed. What would appear to be the main block is over 20ft in length, about 15ft wide and in excess of 5ft in height, with its upper surface almost entirely covered in these strange cup-markings. Several other

Millstones (left) and stonemason's chisel marks (right) at Carr Crags.

Standing stone at Carr Crags.

large slabs form what appears to be a semi-circle about 80ft in diameter behind this huge block — and each of these, too, have a number of the cup-marks engraved on to its surface.

It is possible to detect other stones that may have some significance or connection with this circle, but unfortunately, with the site being heavily quarried, some of the stones may have been buried, or indeed, removed altogether. Also, it is difficult to determine if these stones have, at some time, been stand-ing upright or have always laid flat.

The magic and fascination of this site is that it provides so much material for theoretical interpretation. Masons, miners, farmers and perhaps prehistoric man have all haunted this area. Each of these long-gone groups may well have been able to provide part of the answer to this strange enigma. One thing is certain, though — the remote, wild, windswept Carr Crags will keep its secrets safe for many more hundreds of years.

Dry Stone Walling

DRY stone walls in the upper dales of County Durham help form the familiar hillside patterns of homesteads and enclosures. Most of the walls in the Durham Dales are about 200 years old. Collectively they are said to contain more stone and are longer than the Great Wall of China.

Like most field boundaries these walls resulted from the Acts of Parliament known as the Enclosure Acts. The idea was to improve agricultural efficiency, allowing the management of individual fields and the controlled grazing of livestock. Prior to the Acts, communities farmed the land around their houses in open fields. Each farmer had a strip of land about a furlong (220 yards) in length and 11 yards wide. However, these were not separated by hedges or walls. At the time of the Acts, commissioners were appointed who were given the authority to sell the open fields and commons to pay for the building of walls around the new fields, although in

An example of dry stone walling at Sedling Rake, Weardale.

Alfie Foster practises the art of dry stone walling at Muggleswick (left) and a finished stretch of 'dykeing' at Carr Brow Moor (right).

many cases the buyers were obliged to enclose the land they purchased as part of the contract. For the larger areas the walls were built by teams of specialist itinerant wallers, but for the smaller areas the owners themselves probably built the walls.

Dry stone walling, or 'dykeing', as it is locally called, is a skilful craft and the walls are a wonderful feat of engineering. The usual dimensions are 2ft 4ins wide at the base, tapering to 1ft 4ins wide at the top. They stand 4ft 6ins high and are topped by a 9ins coping, making a total height of 5ft 3ins. When they were originally built, the cost of walling, including quarrying the stone, amounted to two shillings a yard length (about 10p per metre). A competent craftsman could lay up to seven yards a day and would be paid about two shillings for his labour.

Wall building did not begin with the passing of the Enclosure Acts, for building in stone had been a practice for centuries. This craft had evolved over many years and was merely put to new use.

Dry stone walls are built today using exactly the same methods as 200 years ago. The tools used are a spade to dig foundations, a hammer to knock awkward stones into shape, and frames and lines to keep the courses and verticals straight. First, the position of the proposed wall is marked out and the stone acquired. Most of the stone for building the original walls in Durham was quarried. It was usual to use a quarry further up the hill and sledge the stone down — hauling stone up from the valleys would have been a formidable task.

A 4ft-wide bed is then dug for the 'footings', which go on to firm sub-soil or rock. Two rows of large boulders are laid first, their best face out. The space between the rows is filled as the wall rises. This filling is known as the 'heartings' and is placed with care, not just shovelled in. At 2ft high the walls are 'thruffed', by placing large, flat stones right through the wall. The stones are all laid level, not leaning into the wall, the 'batter', or vertical taper is achieved by recessing each course slightly. The courses, however, must all be horizon-

Two hundred years of inclement weather have taken their toll on the stone walling at Race Head.

tal, regardless of the slope of the ground. After a further 2ft are built, another set of thruffs is placed to key the two faces of the wall together. The copings are then placed obliquely along the top of the whole construction and the wall is ready for at least 200 years.

A well-built wall is a splendid piece of engineering, well balanced, flexible and functional. It can move with the ground it stands on but no stone can be moved alone. The dry stone walls have matured with the landscape, working in harmony with nature to provide an extension to the habitat. Mosses and lichen add a rich decoration that is further embellished by wildflowers in spring and summer.

Animals and birds also take advantage of these man-made havens. The weasel, for instance, searches every crevice in the walls for its favourite prey — mice and voles. And the rabbit, of course, will make use of any natural space in the wall as a convenient bolt hole. Insect-eating birds, such as the pied wagtail, find a rich supply here, while other, larger birds find the tops of walls useful for surveying nest sites, or keeping a watchful eye on would-be predators.

Dry stone walls are certainly an attractive feature of the Durham Dales, although their future is by no means certain. A recent survey revealed that 87 per cent of the country's 70,000 miles of dry stone wall were deteriorating or derelict. More than 2,500 miles of wall have disappeared over the past 12 years while almost 12,000 miles are little more than lines on the ground. It costs £30-£40 to repair one metre of wall from scratch, plus an extra £20 if the stone has to be supplied. It would be a shame indeed to lose these miles of stone walls that serve so well as a collective monument to those highly-skilled master masons of yesteryear.

(opposite)
Westerton
observatory
tower, a legacy
of Thomas
Wright.

Southern County Durham

Westerton Tower

SET on the green of this elevated, but little known unspoilt hamlet, two miles east of Bishop Auckland, is a curiously designed stone-built round tower. In Gothic style it is apparently none the worse for its 200 years. Indeed a curiosity, but by no means a folly (as it is sometimes unkindly described), it was designed and built as an observatory by Thomas Wright (1711-85) of the nearby village of Byers Green.

He was quite a remarkable man, variously described as astronomer, architect, author, landscape gardener and mathematician. He was highly respected in his time but is now seemingly forgotten. However, his achievements were almost incredible and certainly inspiring.

Sadly he did not live to benefit from his observatory. He died at Byers Green, his birthplace, in 1785, having settled down there in 1762, as he said, '*to finish my studies*'. His retreat was his own creation, Byers Green Lodge, a mansion set in landscaped grounds with views as far as Durham Cathedral. This country house has long since been swallowed up in industrial development but the observatory and the nearby entrance to the Bishop's Park, at the top of Park Head Bank, remain as two modest examples of his remarkable achievements.

Hett Village

A SLEEPY village surrounding a green of considerable acreage which the world seems to be passing by, and that is how the folk here like it.

Despite its antiquity, Hett has no parish church, having been transferred from the parish of Merrington

The pond in Hett Village.

to Croxdale in 1843. The Methodists built a chapel and William Shepherd, an Evangelist minister, died here in 1873 when only 28 years old, his lifetime's ambitions unfulfilled.

Wandering along the length of the village today, it is difficult to believe that Hett once boasted a small coal mine, a good freestone quarry, seven farms, two public houses and a paper mill on the Tursdale Beck which also ground corn. So much activity, now stilled.

The ducks have to be induced to take to their pond on the green. A natural reaction to 'outsiders', perhaps.

Sorry for intruding. Sleep on, halcyon Hett. Sleep on into yet another century.

Hardwick Hall Park's gothic gatehouse.

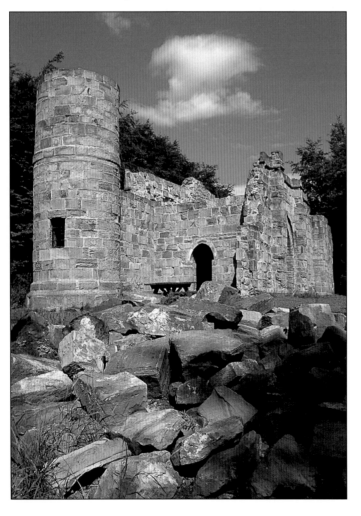

Hardwick Hall Park, Sedgefield

WEST of Sedgefield is Hardwick Hall, originally the family seat of John Burdon. It stands in extensive parkland which is liberally, and indeed, extravagantly, provided with a wide range of follies and landscaped with such grandeur as to even exceed the practice of the period.

Unfortunately this initial extravagance in the 1750s led to Burdon's impoverishment and resulted in his building a house of simple style, quite inappropriate to its setting. Forty acres of lake, excavated in 1754, created a river-like scene within view of the Hall, at one point bridged over by a most elegant ballustraded stone single arch, near to a midstream statue of Neptune.

In the nearby woodland lies a crumbling stone medieval gateway, quite convincing to this day, and all around are remains of banqueting hall, bath house and temple. The Hall is now an hotel but the parkland is a public area in the care of Durham County Council and provides an opportunity to slip into the tranquility of the countryside to enjoy a most pleasant hour or two.

Bishop Middleham Park Wall

MOTORWAY travelling is not the most enjoyable of pastimes and when an interesting feature does occur, it is usually passed in an instant and lost to the memory.

This need not be said of the ancient stone park wall at Bishop Middleham which runs parallel with the A1(M)

eight miles south of Durham City. It was built in the 12th century to establish the boundary of the Bishop's Park surrounding his house or castle. Whilst successive bishops do not appear to have continued in residence beyond the 14th century, the walled park was recorded as being of 70 acres in 1649, by which time there was probably little left of the house.

Surtees tells us, quoting Hunter's Manuscripts, that Bishop James Pilkington (consecrated 1561) *'Gave away many of the stones of the Manor House of Bishop Mydlam and so defaced it.'*

Today the site of the house can be determined by the turf-covered outlines of the remaining walls. These, too, are visible from the motorway but the site is well worth a visit, because it also provides an excellent opportunity to see the unspoilt village with its early 13th-century church.

Ferryhill Windmill

WINDMILLS and watermills have a fascination for many of us and few local examples escape our notice, but Ferryhill Windmill is surely the least known in County Durham. Hidden behind the aged miners' homes at Dean Bank, this towering piece of industrial

archaeology can easily be overlooked by the traveller.

All the 6,000 mills recorded in *Domesday Book* were watermills, for grinding corn, as windmills were not introduced into this country until the late 12th century.

Ferryhill Mill, which ground corn, is, however, much later and calculated to have been built in 1840. Its round, tapering tower is constructed of limestone quarried within a few hundred yards. First recorded in the 1841 Census return as 'Cow Hill Mill' and later as 'Hill House Mill', it appears to have operated as a separate entity with its independent approach from the Merrington Road to its two adjacent cottages, now demolished.

Today, with its 18 acres, it is incorporated into High Hill House Farm. It stands close to the farm's approach road but is fenced off as it is wisely considered to be in a dangerous condition. Much of the masonry below the window openings has collapsed but the tower still stands to its original height. No trace of the rotating cap or the sails survives, although much of the internal timber subframing for the machinery is visible through the fractures in the

The ancient Bishop Middleham Park Wall.

Ferryhill Windmill at Dean Bank.

masonry. It ceased to function sometime between 1897 and 1919, crippled, it is said, by a devastating thunderstorm, and has deteriorated ever since.

Local tradition persistently associates the ruined mill with the triple murder of the Brass children of Hill House Farm, for which Andrew Mills, their father's servant, was executed and hung in chains at 'Mill's Stob' just north of Ferryhill. The truth is, however, that the windmill was not built until many years after this 1692 tragedy.

Cleves Cross

ON the very outskirts of Ferryhill there stands, recently transferred from Cleves Cross Farm, a fragment of a very old stone cross which tradition says was erected about 1200 AD. It marked the slaughtering place of a great wild boar, or brawn, as known at that time, which had terrorised the area from as far afield as Brancepeth.

Cleves Cross, Ferryhill.

The champion was Roger Hodge, who has come down the centuries as Roger De Ferry. Having established the boar's regular track, he dug and disguised a pit to entrap the 'monster', thereby becoming the local hero and earning a place in the history of the county. He was eventually laid to rest in the parish churchyard of Merrington, his grave being marked by a coffin-shaped tombstone carved with spade and sword to commemorate his achievement.

It is difficult to establish when wild boars became extinct in this county. Having provided Roman invaders with their sport, they eventually were protected by law in the 10th and 11th centuries to ensure hunting for lords and bishops in their extensive hunting parks which in Weardale were among the biggest in the country. Struggling to survive, wild boars may have continued into the 17th century.

Bishopton Castle

MOTHER Nature has been quietly busy at Bishopton over the last 800 years. She has draped the collapsed remains of the Conyers' 12th-century castle so gracefully green that the result could be mistaken for man's artistry.

Bishop Ranulf of Durham presented the township of Bishopton to Roger de Conyers sometime in the early 12th century, but since the only rising ground was already occupied by the village, Conyers set about creating his own defensive position.

Typical of Norman castles, this was on the motte and bailey principle, the motte, or mound, being probably higher than now surviving and the bailey enclosing numerous buildings.

Conyers was Constable of Durham Castle but here he lacked such a naturally defensible position. He cleverly adapted the low-lying waterlogged land to become an extension of his earthwork defences and controlled their condition by using the nearby stream to flood the area when necessary.

By this strategy in 1143 he was able to resist the usurper William Comyn, who had virtually conquered the remainder of the Palatinate. Conyers then installed the rightful Bishop, William de St Barbara, in his impenetrable castle, and helped to recover his Palatinate, operating from this stronghold. The castle was never built in stone unlike most motte and bailey castles, such as Durham. Thereby we are fortunate to inherit a totally undeveloped example, the like of which is nowhere to be found in the county.

It was once known by local people as 'Fairy Hill' and we may well have the fairies to thank for the mound's survival. Apparently there was an attempt to cart away the mound and a little voice asked, *"Is all well?" "Yes,"* was the workmen's reply. The little voice continued, *"Then keep well when you are well and leave the Fairy Hill alone."*

The Fairy Hill survives — but do the fairies? There have been no recent reports. Perhaps they have moved on and are working on other threatened sites?

Nature has taken over the remains of Bishopton Castle.

Walworth Castle

A QUITE remarkable building, requiring much deliberation, Walworth Castle was originally built in 1189 by Gilbert Hansard of Neville connection. It remained in that family until sold to

Walworth Castle, now an hotel, was once host to King James VI of Scotland.

Thomas Jennison about 1590, by which time it was partly in ruins. His wealth came from being Auditor-General for Ireland, to Queen Elizabeth. Jennison saved the south front and rebuilt the east and west wings, hence the two splendid Elizabethan elevations adjacent to the earlier south block which terminates in two substantial four-storeyed circular corner towers. It seems probable that the original building comprised four of these towers to complete a quadrangle.

Walworth's greatest day would be 14 May 1603 when Jennison's widow entertained King James VI of Scotland on his journey to London to be crowned James I of England.

World War Two saw Walworth in military use and later housing prisoners-of-war, after which Durham County Council bought it for conversion to a special residential school for girls. In 1981 it became a privately owned hotel.

Walworth village, which lay to the north of the castle and may have been of Saxon origin, began to decline in the early 17th century. Indeed, its demise was probably planned. At that time it was the practice of some wealthy landowners to eliminate obstructions in order to open up new vistas and enable landscaping of parkland and the creation of formal gardens. Villagers were evicted and villages levelled for that purpose.

The fact that the sole survivor of this deserted village is a late Norman chapel may seem to support the supposition that the village was demolished, although sadly for many years now it has been relegated to farm buildings use. Perhaps in these days when farmers are seeking supplementary incomes, the old chapel may be rescued and incorporated into a farm visit enterprise.

Ovington, The Maypole Village

OVINGTON, 'The Maypole Village', sits high above the River Tees, about six miles downstream from Barnard Castle. The huge maypole, possibly the only permanent one left in the county, dominates the village green. It was erected in celebration of Queen Victoria's Diamond Jubilee in 1897 and was said to be made from one of the largest and finest trees on the Raby Estate.

May Day was the beginning of the summer in the Celtic year and modern May celebrations are derived from these old pagan festivities. The first maypole was a tree around which people would dance, clapping their hands to wake the spirit within.

Through the years a green branch came to be used and eventually, a bare pole which could be kept from year to year, for the sake of convenience, served the purpose.

No longer used but a reminder of country traditions, the maypole in Ovington Village.

The Ovington Maypole is no longer used in celebrations but it still stands as a rather sad reminder of a joyous English country tradition.

Gainford Spa

GAINFORD Spa can be reached from a lay-by just west of the village and lies about three quarters of a mile upstream, towards Winston. The route is a pleasant, easy walk along the shaded bank of the River Tees. At the end of the path, just before a rocky outcrop, is the spa itself. It is a mineral water fountain pouring forth from a font-like structure, in a pool, near to the water's edge. These sulphurous springs were very popular in Victorian times because it was believed that drinking the strange-tasting, pungent liquid was beneficial to health and general well-being.

True or not, the presence of the spa led to the building of a number of guest houses in the village, but nothing like on the scale of the hotels in the better-known spa villages of Croft and Dinsdale nearby. The history of the village of Gainford stretches back to a remote period and was first mentioned by Symeon of Durham in 801 AD, but it would seem that there was a monastic establishment on the site prior to this date.

The first church built at Gegnford, as it was then written, was Saxon. It was built in the 9th century by Egelric, who was Bishop of Lindisfarne from 830-845 AD. Egelric is also credited with the construction of the early village which was built on the enclosure style, that is in a square around a village green. Livestock could be driven into this com-

The spa at Gainford.

pound and thus defended against rustlers and outlaws.

Gainford has had many interesting additions over the years, among them the splendid Gainford Hall, a fine example of a Jacobean mansion, which displays all the important architectural features of the era. In the garden is a 17th-century dovecote from which the residents of the Hall would obtain a supply of pigeon eggs — and the main ingredient for pigeon pie — both regarded as great delicacies by the Elizabethans.

High Coniscliffe Church

THIS is said to be the only church in England dedicated to St Edwin, King of Northumbria, although its place name seems to have royal origin. Coniscliffe interprets as Kingcliffe, referring, no doubt, originally to the limestone cliffs along the riverside.

The church was originally built on a limestone ridge, high above the River Tees on the south side of the village street, and its impressive south elevation is accentuated by quarrying having encroached right up to its very boundary wall.

As seen from the village street, St Edwin's sits well behind the building

High Coniscliffe Church, dedicated to St Edwin, King of Northumbria.

Piercebridge Roman Fort

BY 80 AD the Roman invaders had conquered the North of England and were building their Dere Street from York, through County Durham and beyond, towards Scotland. This was a supply route to support their advancing and occupational forces, hence County Durham's other Roman forts on Dere Street — at Binchester, Lanchester and Ebchester.

When the River Tees was encountered, the Roman bridge builders, using their considerable experience in civil engineering gained on the continent, took this in their stride and built a substantial bridge, of stone piers and timber superstructure, downstream from today's stone-arched bridge, and, as was their usual practice, also built a fort to defend this important river crossing.

Today, virtually the whole of the delightful, unspoilt village of Piercebridge is built within, and against, the ramparts of this fort's stone-built successor, and seems to guard the extensive green with all its unexplored treasure. An area within the rampart on the east of the fort has been excavated and is well worth inspection, but there is a quite separate site nearby, which especially deserves to be visited.

In the 2nd century the Roman bridge was swept away and a new crossing site was selected downstream, involving diversions to Dere Street both north and south of the river. Here they built a bridge of enormous abutments and piers in massive stone blocks and heavy timberwork. At this point on the meandering Tees its course is running due west to east, but the river began to encroach on the northern bank, leaving

line, amidst centuries of burials and trees. It is approached through a lych gate which seems to set the scene. The church is very long and narrow, the spired tower, very high. Much of interest takes the eye, from the curious two-storeyed battlemented vestry at the east end, to the gleaming gold weather cock at the west.

The Norman north doorway has survived all the subsequent building work, all the additions, the renovations. It is now well protected by the south porch which has been rebuilt here. The tower stands soundly, without buttresses, even after a stone-clad spire was added unusually early, in the 15th century, proving the wisdom of building on rock.

The excavations of the Roman fort at Piercebridge.

the south abutment and piers silted up and isolated on dry land. Eventually the bridge had to be extended at its northern end and its southern end was converted into a causeway.

It is the recently excavated remains of this bridge which are an outstanding attraction. After the Romans withdrawal, early in the 5th century, the bridge would not be maintained and eventually it collapsed. This and the river's changing course combined to preserve a unique opportunity for us to examine these impressive remains of a Roman bridge on dry land.

These revelations, initiated by river gravel quarrying, serve to remind us of Piercebridge artifacts already recovered from its 1,900-year-old underground treasure store but sadly dispersed to other locations. Who will be brave enough to suggest further excavations at Piercebridge — and shrewd enough to create accommodation so that Piercebridge can display its own treasures?

Sadberge

THE village of Sadberge stands proudly on a hill which affords a commanding view of the countryside between Stockton and Darlington. It has always been a place of considerable importance. The abandoned Roman fort became the site of the Saxon witenagemote, where as many as 100 prelates and officials would meet to discuss judicial affairs and administrative matters for the area between the Tyne and the Tees. Sadberge was a county long before

The stone commemorating the Golden Jubilee of Queen Victoria in Sadberge.

had been detached from the rock in the west and deposited by a glacier.'

The beautiful St Andrew's Church was built in 1831 on a site alongside the previous Norman church, which had, in turn, replaced the original Saxon building. The present church does, however, incorporate some of the earlier relics into its fabric. Perhaps the most interesting of these are two small carved stones built into the walls of the porch. One depicts Adam and Eve in the Garden of Eden and the other bears traces of a carving which may represent Christ trampling on Satan. Strangely, these items were recovered from a Darlington inn. The materials from the ancient church were sold for the princely sum of £10 and most of the stone was used to provide an embankment for the River Skerne, the rest being used in the building of the kitchen of the Glittering Star in Darlington, but thanks to sober vigilance the carved stones were returned to their rightful place.

Durham. Indeed, its earldom is still one of the titles attached to the Crown. One of its rare uses can be seen on the plaque on the huge glacial erratic found on the village green. It reads:

> 'This stone was placed here to commemorate the jubilee of Queen Victoria, Queen of the United Kingdom, Empress of India and Countess of Sadberge, June 20th 1887. It was found 12 feet below the surface in making the reservoir. It

Timothy Hackworth Museum, Shildon

TIMOTHY Hackworth is one of the underrated pioneers of railway history. He was born in Wylam, near Newcastle on 22 December 1786. He became a blacksmith at the local colliery and by 1807 had risen to the rank

of foreman, like his father before him. It was at Wylam that he helped build Hedley's locomotives to run on the level 5ft gauge railway there. In 1815 he left Wylam after a dispute about Sunday working and moved briefly to Walbottle, only a few miles away. Following this he worked at Stephenson's Forth Street Works in Newcastle before he took up the position of resident engineer at Shildon, to the Stockton & Darlington Railway, on 28 June 1825.

During this time George Stephenson was frequently away on other railway schemes and the task of maintaining the company's five existing steam engines fell to Timothy Hackworth. It was here that he built the *Royal George*, the first six-coupled locomotive and the first on which the cylinders drove directly on to the wheels. It entered service in November 1827 and was so suc-

cessful that it was the forerunner of several further heavy engines he produced for the railway, typified by the *Wilberforce* and *Majestic* classes of engine.

The Globe, a four-coupled engine with inside cylinders, followed in 1829. This engine was built specially for passenger and light goods work. It was used for the opening of the Middlesbrough branch of the railway on 27 December 1830. It was during the construction of this branch that Timothy Hackworth won a company award of 150 guineas for his design of coal staithes, which he was then asked to build.

He took over the Shildon Works from the Stockton & Darlington Railway in 1833 and contracted to maintain their engines and work their traffic. At Shildon in 1836 he built a locomotive for the St Petersburg Railway, the first

The Timothy Hackworth Railway Museum, Shildon.

engine to run in Russia, and in 1837 he built the *Samson* for the Albion Mines in Nova Scotia, one of the first engines to run in Canada.

Timothy Hackworth is probably best known for his engine *Sanspareil*, which he entered in the Rainhill Locomotive Trials in 1829, to find the best locomotive on the London & Manchester Railway. His main competitor, and the eventual winner, was Robert Stephenson's *Rocket*. Hackworth suffered bad luck — his engine was 5cwt too heavy for the competition. However, it was allowed to enter but broke down during the trials. It was repaired and kept working until 1844 and in 1863 was put on display in the Science Museum in London.

In 1840 Hackworth resigned from the Stockton & Darlington Railway to develop his own Soho Engine Works at Shildon. It was here in 1849 that he built what he considered to be his masterpiece — *Sanspareil No 2*. It had several new ideas, such as a welded boiler and other innovations incorporated into the design.

Hackworth was not only one of the leading engineers in the pioneering days of the steam locomotive, but his talents also extended to every variation of the skill. He improved the efficiency of the steam boiler, he developed the

'plug wheel' which cut down on breakages, he introduced the spring safety valve and the return tube boiler. He was the first to use lap on the slide valve to make use of the expansive property of steam. He remodelled the winding engines at Brusselton and the Etherley Incline, to improve the lowering and raising of trucks.

Besides being an excellent engineer, he was also a member and preacher of the Wesleyan Society, and he was well known as a devout Christian and philanthropist. Timothy Hackworth died on 7 July 1850. He was, without doubt, one of the most skilful and talented of

Sanspareil, entered in the Rainhill Locomotive Trials, beaten by Stephenson's Rocket.

the engineers of the Industrial Revolution.

The Timothy Hackworth Museum, in his own house at Shildon, not only presents a review of this great man's achievements, but also affords a glimpse at everyday life in Victorian northern England.

'Locomotion' and the Stockton & Darlington Railway

THE *Locomotion* was the first locomotive to run on the history-making

Stockton & Darlington Railway. It was built by George Stephenson who came to be known as 'The Father of Railways'. He was born in Wylam, in Northumberland, on 9 June 1781 and went on to serve his engineering apprenticeship with local collieries while learning to read and write in his spare time. Stephenson invented a miners' safety lamp in 1815 and his inventive mind and engineering skill led to his eventual appointment as engineer to the Stockton & Darlington Railway in 1821. Together with Edward Pease and Thomas Richardson he established the firm of Robert Stephenson & Company in 1823, in Newcastle-upon-Tyne. Robert, his only son, who was born in 1803, was appointed manager of the new company. The success of the Stockton & Darlington Railway bred more success for the Stephensons. They won the £500 first prize at the Rainhill Trials with their locomotive *The Rocket*. George Stephenson eventually rose to be the President of the Institute of Mechanical Engineers, an organisation in which he was to remain active all his life. He died at the age of 65 in 1846.

Robert Stephenson became one of the most respected engineers in the world, achieving great fame for his bridge building, which was to set standards for years to come. In his later years he served as MP for Whitby, in North Yorkshire. He died in 1859 at the age of 56.

This most remarkable father and son team had a lasting and monumental effect on the Industrial Revolution, on a worldwide scale.

The *Locomotion* is the prize exhibit of the North Road Station Railway

The history-making Locomotion, North Road Station Railway Museum.

Museum. This world-famous engine hauled the first train on the opening day of the Stockton & Darlington Railway on 27 September 1825. The engine was built at the Forth Road Works, Newcastle, by the Robert Stephenson Company. It was delivered by road and placed on the tracks at Heighington Station, ready for the opening day. *Locomotion* hauled a train of wagons with 80 tons of coal and carriages full of engineers and committee men over the distance of 18 miles at speeds of 15 to 20 miles per hour. This event had a huge impact on the town of Darlington, which came to be known as the 'Birthplace of Railways'.

The town's other claim to fame is that of having a large Quaker community, and it was a member of that fraternity, Edward Pease (1767-1858), who was the champion of the railway engine as a means of transporting the Durham coal from the coalfields in the west of the county to Teesmouth for shipping to London and the Continent. This effectively cheapened the price of coal, thus making the industry more competitive. Pease supported George Stephenson totally and ensured that the railway triumphed over a counter-proposal to build a canal for coal transportation.

Darlington became established as the railway centre of the world and

skilled craftsmen built locomotives in the town for almost 150 years, until 1966, when the workshops were closed. The town's railway heritage lives on in the North Road Station Railway Museum; it houses one of the finest collections of railway history in the North of England. Engines, rolling stock and other artefacts are all well displayed in this carefully restored Victorian railway station.

Hurworth's Eccentric Mathematician

THE village of Hurworth seems quite unspoilt, its broad and lengthy green separating many admirable examples of domestic architecture, erected over the recent centuries. It also provides a fine setting for the parish church with its burial ground mounted high above the winding Tees, and so offering a vantage point from which to view the river and Yorkshire, beyond.

Hurworth has long been remembered as the life-long home of the eccentric mathematician, William Emerson, (1701-82), whose gravestone, now removed to the western porch, tells its story in Hebrew and Latin. The site of his home, by the edge of the green, has now been re-used but bears a plaque, indicating its famous earlier occupant. If only these present-day buildings could tell their history, and that of their sites over the centuries.

William Emerson was indeed a character, the like of whom we do not meet today. There is much to be gleaned from the memoir prefixed to his work *Mechanics*, republished after his death.

He was born here in 1701, the son of

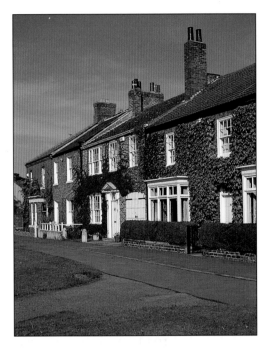

the village schoolmaster from whom, assisted by the curate who lodged with them, he gained more than an elementary education.

But by the time he had reached his late teens he was not content with this and took himself off to extend his knowledge under masters at Newcastle and York. Upon returning to Hurworth he kept a school for a while.

Some time after marrying the rector's niece, and finding the promised dowry of £500 not forthcoming, the matter was raised, whereupon the rector denied any such intention and scorned Emerson most contemptuously. This spurred him into proving that he was the better of the two and he set about achieving this superiority over the course of the next ten years, eventually becoming accepted as one of the greatest mathematicians of the time. He published many acclaimed works on mathematics and science which included navigation and optics. He acquired a general knowledge of music, medicine, and most other sciences.

All this dedication to study took its toll on Emerson and he developed into an eccentric by virtue of his shabby, outdated clothing and peculiar behaviour, sometimes wearing his clothing back to front in winter to prevent the cold penetrating to his chest, but always displaying some other strange whim or bizarre fancy, too.

So, like many great men, Emerson had his faults and peculiarities but it seems they were well outweighed by his virtues, for beneath the grotesque appearance and the hasty temper there beat a truly humane heart which happily helped any deserving fellow creature.

He was therefore respected by the intelligent as a learned man, although the illiterate thought him to be some sort of fortune teller because of his superhuman knowledge. Magical powers were attributed to him by some, and it sometimes suited him to let the ignorant believe so.

He rejected the honour of Fellowship of The Royal Society, believing that a man who had burned so many farthing candles, in study, as he had done, should not then have to pay so much a year for the honour of having FRS after his name. Emerson died in 1782 and his widow two years later. They had no children.

Such characters made a great contribution to our development over 200 years ago, and should not be forgotten. Walking through Hurworth today it is quite easy to imagine it is two centuries ago and Emerson's view up and down the green would not be so very different from what we see today, when there are no modern vehicles passing through, of course.

The Hell Kettles

IN A FIELD just north of where the River Skerne meets the Tees at Croft, is what may be County Durham's most intriguing natural phenomenon.

The Hell Kettles, two round pools, each of approximately 30 yards diameter, have always contained sulphurated water and ever since their formation, have been the source of fear and superstition.

Over the centuries, astonishing accounts have accumulated, too numerous to list here, but Abbot Brompton of Jervaux recorded that on Christmas Day 1179: '*The ground rose up to such a height that it was equal to the tops of the highest hills and so remained at that height from nine in the morning till sunset. But at the setting sun the earth fell in with a horrid crash that all that saw that strange mound and heard its fall were so amazed, that for very fear many died, for the earth swallowed up that mound and where it stood there was a deep pool.*'

Some geologists think an explosion may have been caused by the build-up of gases and water in large cavities in the Magnesian Limestone rock. An alternative explanation is that the Hell Kettles could be glacially formed, large pieces of ice having been forced down into glacial debris, forming, as the ice melts, a closed lake. The water becomes rich in minerals from the rocks. Eventually plants colonise the area and the lake gradually fills up with decayed plant material. This would account for the number of ponds reducing from four as recorded in *Murray's Handbook*

Blackwell's Hell Kettles.

of Durham & Northumberland published in 1873.

The air of mystery continues with observers claiming that the water levels never vary in drought or flood conditions. This in turn seems to demolish the tradition that there is a subterranean connection with the Tees.

Despite the strange forces said to lure to a watery death any living creature venturing too close, it seems we should not be deterred from further investigating this fascinating site.

Sockburn — and the Worm

SOCKBURN is significant in the history of County Durham. It was here, on the southernmost tip of the diocese, that the Lords of Sockburn met the incoming Prince Bishop midstream in the Tees to present the Conyers' Falchion with due ceremony. This act was last performed in April 1826 when the county's last Prince Bishop, William van Mildert, entered his Palatinate. The tradition perished with the end of his rule.

The location of Sockburn, on a secluded peninsula formed by the River Tees, provides the backdrop for a fascinating legend: the story of the Sockburn Worm, a legend that is similar to that of the Lambton Worm. At the time

The eerie remains of All Saints' Church, Sockburn.

of the Crusades this area was a misty, marshy land and was terrorised by a '*worm, dragon or fiery flying serpent*', causing devastation and destruction. This worm would feed upon cattle, sheep and pigs and men, women and children — no living thing was safe from its voracious appetite. Its scent was so dreadful that no one could stand it and with the rampage of this terrible creature the land fell barren and famine and desperation were heaped upon its unfortunate inhabitants. Sir John Conyers, the Lord of the Manor of

Conyers' Chapel (left) and (right) the Greystone, keeping the Sockburn Worm in its final resting place.

Sockburn Hall, built on the site of the original Conyers' Manor House.

Sockburn, felt sorrow for his people and swore to do something about this fearsome beast. Many men had tried to kill this huge, awesome worm but had been killed, or at least terribly maimed or seriously injured.

Sir John put on his full armour and went into All Saints' Church. In the silence of the family chapel he prayed for help in trying to rid his lands of the worm. He prayed all night and such was his belief in the power of the Lord that he offered up his only son to the Holy Ghost.

At first light, filled with confidence, Sir John took up the family sword — The Conyers' Falchion — a huge yard-long, curved broadsword that had seen many bloody battles. He awaited the return of the worm to its lair. When it appeared a dreadful combat ensued, Sir John's faith and trust in the Lord helped him wield the mighty weapon with divine skill and deadly accuracy, and after a long and desperate struggle he struck off the head of the vile creature. Sir John immediately knelt in prayer to give thanks. At the news of the worm's death people came from their homes. They were overjoyed and sang and danced for the first time in years. However, before they partook of a huge feast, Sir John had them dig a deep pit and push into it the body of the worm. In fear of it rising from the dead they capped the pit with a great boulder. This stone, the Greystone as it is known, can still be seen today.

On hearing the story, the King granted the Manor of Sockburn to the Conyers family forever and decreed that the symbol of their ownership, the mighty Conyers' Falchion, should be presented to each new Prince Bishop as he rode across the Tees at Sockburn ford. This magnificent sword is now on display in Durham Cathedral.

Apart from the sword, everything connected with the legend is still on the original site, which is, however, private land.

Sockburn Hall replaced the original Conyers Manor House and nearby are the remains of All Saints' Church. Evidence suggests the church was established before the Norman Conquest but the visible remains today are from the 12th, 14th and 19th centuries. The restored Conyers Chapel on the north nave is preserved as a small museum and contains incised medieval slabs,

Saxon crosses and some fine examples of some pre-Conquest 'Hogback' gravestones. The figure of a cross-legged knight with chain coiff is believed by some historians to be that of Sir John Conyers, slayer of the worm.

The huge, uninscribed, flat rock that is a tombstone to the worm can be seen in a nearby field, although again, this is private land.

This area at the southern tip of the peninsula is a wonderfully unspoilt, evocative place, full of atmosphere — a place where it is easy to believe in the legend of the Sockburn Worm. Stand awhile and listen. Can you be sure that the dry rustle of the leaves and undergrowth is caused only by the wind?

Index